GOOD

BRINKWORTH

**SO GOOD
SO FAR**

BRINKWORTH SO GOOD SO FAR

GRAEME BROOKER

LUND HUMPHRIES

CONTENTS

FOREWORD

PETER HIGGINS

This is an extremely timely book.
Traditional retail is collapsing, the spectre of Brexit and economic crisis looms whilst inexplicably interior design and architecture courses continue to proliferate, sending students out into this volatile marketplace. It is because of such uncontrollable situations that as designers we need help to consolidate and define our function in order to justify our futures.

Why is it that the basic essence and role of the interior designer has been neglected for so long. Maybe it's because every homebuilder imagines that they are one, fuelled by instantaneous and gratifying digital snapshots, the lure of the (diminishing) world of glossy magazines or parachuting into Salone del Mobile in Milan. In response to this, the craft of design needs to be deconstructed and synthesised which is exactly what this book does in the context of two highly talented and committed practitioners.

Directors of design practices are really just like football mangers (in the case of Brinkworth player-managers) who attract and gather the best possible talent around them and then apply their idiosyncratic and carefully refined alchemy. But fellow design principals would ask, 'that's OK but how do you then empower your team to improvise, experiment and play at another level'? Somehow Adam Brinkworth and Kevin Brennan, with colleagues' endorsements talking of family, inclusivity, a creative culture that is generous, open, honest and free. Nobody seems to own an idea they just want the best.

The book forensically penetrates the growth of a practice not only through the work but also by demonstrating an understanding of critical design methodologies; what is a client, what is a product, what is a raw broken-down site, what is a narrative and how do you stimulate and build a team around you that will inherit your passion and help resolve and share the best solution?

Here we have a superb example of how these defining criteria have been successfully balanced and articulated in practice through intelligence and sensitivity but always realistically controlled in the shadow of a self-imposed rigour of trial, error and risk. The startling quantity, unquestionable quality and extreme diversity of their typologies including retail, workplace, even a skate park to a reservoir residence, demonstrate a furtive eye for projects and has been hard won.

As if that's not enough then Adam and Kevin go further, much further than most. The end product is not just handed over. They energise clients to reinvent and populate their spaces and brands not only through design but also through an uncanny sense of inhabited space, which they allow to evolve and respond to the people that own and use them. This may be activated through extended relationships and consequential evolutions of ideas 'in practice' for both themselves and their clients. They see how design can genuinely facilitate the overused concept of place making but at the same time have a fundamental understanding of how important it is to encourage clients and investors to support and value creativity in order to develop successful shop, live-work and play experiences.

This is not just a retrospective study, it also encourages us to ask where do they go now? There is evidence that both Adam and Kevin are mindful of the seismic shift in the retail world as products are available with just a tap of a device to be delivered by drones. Thankfully Brinkworth's response is to do two things: value and promote 'The Power of the Real' in the age of the virtual, where tangible products and spaces provide opportunities for all of us to meet, communicate, empathise and participate and at the same time exploit and embed the potential of the digital domain.

If you are ever thinking of commissioning Brinkworth or becoming a practitioner in their studio be prepared to undertake an enthralling rollercoaster ride within a team that will understand and embrace the maker's craft, materiality, detail, space making and product narrative alongside the fascinating and growing mercurial world of sensors, algorithms, augmentation and code.

FOREWORD

MICHAEL MARRIOTT

I first met Adam at a birthday party on a Thames riverboat, not long after I'd left college. We then met again at some design event, and at some point started meeting up more regularly, usually to see art, which most of the time then led on to a bar and more discussion of design and art, amongst other things. During this period we had both been working from home and were both at the stage where we felt it was time to find a studio, so the idea of sharing a space took shape. Not long after, I came across a semi-derelict building in Bethnal Green, near where I lived. It was the ground floor of a brick coach house, full of old carpet samples and dead pigeons, but it was a good size, with lots of potential and big enough for both studio and workshop space, which we both wanted. Eventually we secured a lease, borrowed a van to get rid of the bits of carpet, pigeons and other debris, and started to make it into a studio.

Once we were working in the same space, I inevitably got to know Adam much better. One of the things that impressed me was the vigorous way he approached work, combining super-practical problem-solving with a unique vision for a space and client that belied all its practicality, expediency and budget. The majority of early projects were stores for Karen Millen. Karen Millen was still a young company with just a handful of shops, but it was also an ambitious and energetic enterprise. Adam had fallen into working for them almost by chance, but proved to be a vital partner: a relationship that enabled their brisk growth. A key part of their nimbleness was Adam's agility as a designer, enabling them to launch exciting new stores at an incredible rate. A typical project would start with a phone call from the client to announce a deal on a new site and that keys would be available the following day!

The first site visit would therefore include a hastily assembled wrecking crew, to clear out whatever was left of any previous fit out. Adam would be there, hammer in hand, searching for what was behind existing surfaces, measuring up and starting to rough out a plan. Whilst ripping out was finishing up, Adam would be back at the drawing board, designing and planning, usually in a way that could incorporate a maximum off-site fabrication. This whirlwind process enabled elements to be ready to be installed on site almost as soon as the skip had removed unwanted elements, and whilst services were being installed.

Another factor that made this speed possible was that it was a small tight team. The client trusted Adam to get on with the job and deliver a beautiful, seamless result, on time and on budget. Adam meanwhile organised the projects in the fashion of a design and build unit, with a small team of regular and reliable collaborators and sub-contractors. Despite the breath-taking speed of installation of new shops, solutions were innovative, befitting of the existing space and the clients' needs, and often with supremely inventive ways of satisfying conservative planning requirements at the same time: all were done with a furious enthusiasm.

During the time we shared the space, the rate of new projects and clients gathered pace. It was fast enough that during our first year there, personnel expanded from just one to half a dozen or so, helping to manage what had become a constant flow of work. At some point I moved out, and Brinkworth continued to expand into the rest of the space, adding staff as projects required.

Several of the growing Brinkworth team were friends first, or have become friends along the way, including, notably, co-director Kevin Brennan, who we both met around the same time, during a period when Shoreditch was a kind of hub for creative East London. Some of the team have worked for Brinkworth, left, then returned again once they realised which side their toast was buttered!

Along the way they have renovated the building itself and taken over the first floor too. Together, Kevin and Adam seem determined to ensure the studio, however it grows or evolves, retains the feel of a group of friends heading out on a weekend together. The family ethos of the studio and its professionalism, together with Adam's love of all things skate, surf or hot rod and Kevin's love of brutal Corbusian bunkers, have established a thriving and energetic team that slowly expands along with the client base and project types (but which is a number that is held in check by the seating capacity of Pellicci's café!).

I have more recently, via a collaborative project for BIRD, a fried chicken restaurant, become re-acquainted with the Brinkworth machine. This has given me an insight into how the team has grown alongside the breadth of projects, clients and collaborators (including Stafford Schmool, Ben Kelly and the Wilson Brothers). When I was first approached to work on BIRD, my immediate thought was that we needed Brinkworth in on this. On a purely practical level, I knew they had the capacity to project manage and roll out the scheme into the future, but I also felt they had the experience and sensitivity to be able to work in a creative collaboration successfully. Part of this was the fact that I knew them already and what they were capable of, but I think there's also a genuine enthusiasm and openness, seeing each new project or collaboration as an opportunity to do good work, inject more energy and keep the motor running sweetly. As always, it was a joy to work with them.

This book is a testament not just to the ground-breaking work they have done but it is also a demonstration of the uniqueness of the practice. It has been a pleasure to introduce it with my recollections of my relationship with them.

INTRODUCTION

THINKING AND MAKING

If I was to sum up Brinkworth, it probably wouldn't be a handshake, it would be a hug.
OSCAR WILSON, WILSON BROTHERS

Since 1990, when Adam Brinkworth initiated his practice with his first furniture commission for the Karen Millen clothes shop in London, the company has realised over 2,500 projects in more than 80 countries. 'This means that, in the practice's 28-year existence, a building project has been completed approximately every 90 hours. The astounding frequency of finished work appears counter-intuitive to the title of this chapter: how does anybody have time to think, let alone make, at this pace of output?

Brinkworth design all kinds of interior spaces. Much of their work focuses on the design of retail spaces. Retail design is an industry powered by efficient delivery, typified by modularised roll-out, and epitomised by the chain store. In this context, they are unique. Brinkworth are not interested in the mass production of interior spaces. Their inclination is to always make the time to think, and then to make informed and appropriate responses to their clients' and collaborators' requirements that are distinctive and inimitable. Alongside their work in retail, the completed restaurants, bars, hotels, exhibitions, workspaces and residential environments are equally as thoughtful, innovative and stimulating. All of their work is one-off, bespoke and delivered with an intelligence that infuses the carefully considered requirements of the client with the vagaries of a particular site. In short, Brinkworth originate and make spaces that redefine how we shop, live, work and play.

This chapter will offer an insight into their work and what drives its inception and delivery. It is called 'Thinking and Making' because this simple concept defines the unique culture of the Brinkworth approach to the design of space. Their processes of work, the history of the company and the culture that has evolved are all part of a unique synthesis of people, place and identity: all of which are filtered through the extensive processes of intelligent thinking and the thoughtful and sophisticated responses to those ideas through their making.

In order to fully understand the Brinkworth cultures, we must start at the beginning of the company's formation.

If I was going to do it again, I would probably change the name... ADAM BRINKWORTH IN A LECTURE TO INTERIOR DESIGN STUDENTS AT THE RCA, 7 NOVEMBER 2017

To be honest I've never even thought about it, it's never bothered me, Adam's really good at being Brinkworth.
KEVIN BRENNAN

Adam's casual remark, made at the start of a presentation to a room full of design students, conveyed a critical insight into the culture and values of Brinkworth. Evident in the many interviews and conversations undertaken with the practice and its clients is the sense of openness and engagement engendered in the company. It is an atmosphere of cooperation, encouraged by all of its employees. All interviewees enjoyed an egalitarian approach to the work and were committed to how it was undertaken. In short, passionate engagement from all participants in all aspects of Brinkworth work is a given. Egos are not. Teams are formed around work as it comes into the office, and all participants are invited to be open, honest and free with their contributions. The best ideas often win. So, why the name?

I called it Brinkworth, because it was only ever going to be me and I admired other furniture designers like the Eames's and so on. They just used their name.
ADAM BRINKWORTH

Rather than constrain the practice the name has proved instrumental in its development.

Then, what I found by employing other people, was that it was incredibly liberating, because they had lots of different strengths and weaknesses, and you could produce great things. I still care very much about how it's perceived, and what gets produced here, but I'm liberated in some respects, because loads of great stuff comes out of here, and it doesn't even have to have me do a thing on it.
ADAM BRINKWORTH

How did the practice begin? An undergraduate degree in furniture design in Wolverhampton, followed by a master's degree in furniture design at the Royal College of Art (RCA), meant that Adam Brinkworth avoided the conventional interior design based route into industry. This trajectory fostered an approach that relied on the fundamental importance of designing elements and then being able to make them: a philosophy that has remained a core value and integral principle in the practice's ambitions and methodologies. It is an ethos that is based on realisation: if you cannot understand how you make a space, an object, then how can you make it in the manner by which you want it to be utilised?

As important as a profound understanding of making spaces that realise client's ideas, the formation of a suitably representative interior studio in which to house the practice has always been a fundamental requirement of the Brinkworth ethos. A practice space that reflects the values and perspectives of its occupants will demonstrate the ability to interpret client's ideas for their own spaces. Their studio in Bethnal Green has been their home for 25 years. It is a vibrant, hive of activity on two floors. The ex-book-binders workshop, replete with West Ham and QPR colours painted on its columns, a reminder of the partners' favourite football teams, has a backroom filled with motorbikes and is a space with a three-dog rota. It was initially rented with furniture designer, Michael Marriott. The old timber loading bay of the workshop still bears both their names, painted on the doors, and kept ever since: a subtle reminder of the inception of the practice.

It is an active space with people toing and froing, dogs shuffling between feet and, quite often, large greasy motorbikes being wheeled in and out through the front door. It is a professional yet informal environment, one that has an underlying focus of the work being undertaken. It is a faithful representation of the company and its values: busy, studious, concentrated, yet relaxed. It hums with activity, yet it is open and welcoming. It was not always so straightforward. The first Brinkworth studio was in a railway arch in King's Cross, London, and was shared with another RCA alumnus Konstantin Grcic. It was the first studio space, but business was quiet:

I had a design studio. I bought a calculator, and some pens and paper … but didn't have any work. ADAM BRINKWORTH

Trips to Arundel in Sussex to work as a blacksmith three days a week, joining the Enterprise Allowance Scheme and the unforeseen enforced relinquishing of the studio arch meant that the early years of the practice were tough. Furniture commissions were hard to come by and, when they did, the small flat Adam was occupying in South London had to be converted into a workshop. A situation that, when the space was intermittently lined out with plastic sheeting to keep it clean, made the neighbours uneasy:

I think they thought they were living next to a serial killer.
ADAM BRINKWORTH

Early formation of the practice hinged upon one key moment. Motivated by seeing some of the wrought-iron work in Jigsaw stores, Kevin Stanford, the fashion designer Karen Millen's partner, contacted Neil Stephens, the blacksmith in Arundel. His enquiry about making some fittings for their stores in Guildford and the Kings Road in London was passed onto Adam. He met Stanford on site and recalls:

I brought my student portfolio and a chair I had made and Kevin looked at my work and he went, 'Oh I like those. I'll just have my shop like that, please.' He said, 'How much is the whole shop going to be?'

Unprepared for the question Brinkworth said he would respond later. But in order to cement the beginnings of the relationship Stanford made a surprising and generous offer. Brinkworth recollects:

Kevin said, 'In good faith, I'm going to write you a cheque for £1,000.' At the time, I had gone up to my maximum overdraft of £3,000. That week I picked up fruit off the floor in the market because I had no money. I had nothing. I was like, 'Fucking hell £1,000'. That was the end of the meeting pretty much. The next day I gave him a price of £8,400 and he said, 'do it for seven and a half, and I'm going to give you the balance on the second shop you do for me'. I thought 'I bet I never see that.'

The Kings Road store opened in four weeks and, impressed by what he saw, Kevin Stanford not only commissioned Adam to do the next one, but he also paid him the balance of the first project. More importantly, it led to the formation of a very particular early working pattern based around the design of the shop furniture and then its subsequent fitting. This process became fully established when, emboldened by his initial successes, and when becoming frustrated at the lack of accuracy between site information and his furniture designs, in a phone call to Kevin Stanford, Brinkworth suggested he undertake the whole shop fit:

I'd arrive and say, 'The walls aren't straight.' I'd spend ages scribing all my furniture because the furniture was arrow straight. I had unrealistic ambitions that the space I was getting was the same as the drawings they were sending. I phoned Kevin up and said, 'I'm not going to be finished, they're five days late, and I'm waiting here with my furniture.' So Kevin said, 'Well, you do it all then.'

Both moments were acts of generosity that forged a strong bond of trust. It was the beginning of an extensive and successful business partnership: a working partnership that has subsequently resulted in 400 individual stores being delivered across 60 countries. It is one of the longest and most successful partnerships in the retail industry.

This partnership led not only to the nascent origins of Brinkworth as a company, but also initiated the future practice's processes: a method that was hard-boiled through the relentless design, making, delivery and repeat schedule. It was a process that was repeated numerous times as Karen Millen rolled out internationally. Each store was different, responding to the place it was in and the people it wanted to attract. Sometimes each project required unusual approaches in order to get it completed.

We travelled around some of the country designing Karen Millen shops and of course trainer shopping, staying in B&Bs with the builders and sketching ideas while on site. We went out in the evenings with the electricians, plumbers and carpenters. All sketches and drawings had to be done in a Daler A4 layout pad, these were numbered in the right-hand corner, Adam was insistent that the books where the same and the numbering correct. I still have all my sketch books today. The Brinkworth design process in those days was to work together, come up with a style, sketch and make full size mock-ups of some of the furniture. Another role was pretending to be Karen Millen when we had to order the phone and fax lines for a newly built shop, ridiculously only Karen Millen herself was able to place this order, as it turned out this was my five minutes of fame as the starstruck BT operator would ask me questions and tell me how much she admired me and my shops.

SACHA KEMP-PORTER, FIRST EMPLOYEE

The practice was formed.

A second significant event in the origins of the practice took place seven years after the company had been set up. In the Karen Millen Neal Street store in Covent Garden, London, whilst out shopping with his then girlfriend, Kevin Brennan was surprised, as well as relieved, to be sitting in a Matthew Hilton Balzac chair. He recalls:

I was comfy. That night we went to a party in Hoxton and I was speaking to (Michael) Marriott and he said, 'What have you been doing?' I said, 'I went shopping.' He was like, 'Really?', 'Yes, I went to this cracking Karen Millen shop.' … Michael said, 'My mate did that.'

Designer Kevin Brennan had extensive experience in interior practices, such as Ben Kelly Design and Stephen Donald Associates, where he had designed bars, restaurants and clubs. When Michael Marriott introduced Kevin and Adam to each other, they both recognised a kindred spirit. Adam recalls:

When I met Kevin, he was with Ben Kelly. I thought he was an architect. My company had just completed this project, a really daft skateboard bowl, elliptical shop front in the Kings Road. Ben said to me 'You do furniture, leave fucking buildings alone,' and that was the first thing he ever said to me. I thought, who are these people? They turned out to be two of the loveliest, rudest people I've ever met.

It was a pivotal moment. It was a meeting that was to set the practice up for the next 20 years.

I think, culturally, we were coming from the same no-nonsense background. Kevin brought professionalism to the business and process, and he brought the ability to do projects away from retail. ADAM BRINKWORTH

Adam had been working relentlessly for eight years on a very particular schedule of completing Karen Millen stores all over the UK, often from the back of a van, fitting on site as quickly as possible in order to ensure that stores could open quickly and start to make money, before moving onto the next one, keeping the team working. The new partnership and the relentless work schedule meant that something had to change.

I felt a responsibility in that I had keep the guys working on site. I needed to plan ahead, and be getting on with the next project, the next build. All of my working processes at that time were based on how you build something and deliver something quickly. ADAM BRINKWORTH

Restrictions in this approach meant that the company could only realise a certain scale of work – they could not deliver small or interesting low-fee work, hampering innovation or experimentation, or larger projects with a bigger build.

21

We could only deliver spaces that were 250,000 to a million quid, and that precluded a lot of stuff. We were starting to work internationally. We were also working with larger clients by then, and they didn't want us to build it.
ADAM BRINKWORTH

The unyielding schedule that for the first eight years had produced numerous spaces was not only unsustainable but had exposed the practice to unnecessary financial risk. Most significantly it was impeding opportunities to research and explore new processes, materials and methods. Yet it had inculcated the practice with a formidable process-based approach to the thinking and then making of interior space. Brinkworth had not only developed an obsession with making and materiality, but they also had an extensive knowledge of how to assemble space in order to realise their clients' very specific requirements in a very short period of time. It is an understanding that has been a significant aspect of the practice ever since. But the designing and then fitting could not continue.

I realised other people could make things better, less expensively, and also, I wasn't a slave to the machines that I had, so I could muck around with alternative materials and processes. ADAM BRINKWORTH

The relentless production of space had left a lasting legacy. It was an indelible imprint on the way the practice worked. It had produced a distinctive culture in the practice, one that still permeates everything that they now do: it is one of intelligent expedient thinking and then an understanding of how those ideas are realised and delivered.

For me they stand out in that they focus on detailing. They're very good at understanding a client and a brief, or building a brief perhaps with a client; determining what the needs are. Designing for them and making every project specific to the needs of them. MICHAEL MARRIOTT

Materiality is everything. There is an honesty to everything we do. If you look at the Netherall Garden house for instance, the brick house we've just built, it's all about the brick, about the scale and proportion and exposure of the steel frame that supports it. KEVIN BRENNAN

The final space is a real thing. It is a living, breathing, you can touch it feel it, interact with it, so making sure the materiality is considered, as well as the concept, are the two bits for me. It's the idea. We hope it's an idea that's understandable, that's simple, and that it's a really well crafted piece. I don't believe you can design something successfully without understanding what its physical incarnation will be. ADAM BRINKWORTH

A process-based understanding permeates Brinkworth's culture. Originated in their beginnings, they make time to think, and then formulate and assemble a space, with which to demonstrate its meaning and its making.

PRINCIPLES AND PROCESSES

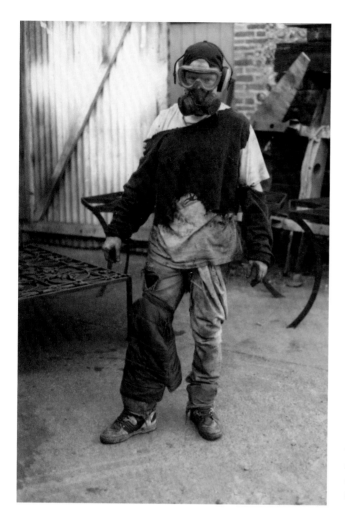

I think you pick it up, don't you? As soon as you walk in the door. It's relaxed yet full of energy.
LUCY PORTER, PR MANAGER

Before this interview, I wrote in my notes: 'no house style'. Culture, 'Relaxed, hardworking, fear and frolic'.
ADAM BRINKWORTH

In Chapter 1, 'Thinking and Making', the origins of the company and how it has informed the various strands of their culture were examined. In order to fully comprehend the Brinkworth philosophy, this chapter charts how the staff, clients and collaborators work, what they value and what they consider to be the essential elements and components of both the principles and the processes of their culture.

PRINCIPLES

Trust. There's no business without trust. We want to think the best of people, and we want to deliver something of meaning. ADAM BRINKWORTH

Forged from their origins as creative people, who not only designed but also built the spaces they were commissioned to formulate, it is fair to say that there is a robust obsession with making which lies at the heart of the company's culture. Brinkworth's formation as the innovators and then manufacturers has led to the obsession of being able to understand and then produce their ideas. These are fundamental principles that by extension encompass an openness of approach to work, an open culture where staff, clients and collaborators are treated as equals. It is an attitude that extends to their play too: *fear and frolic*.

Ad and Kev always winced when we introduced them as our bosses, and I understand why. Brinkworth is so intrinsically intertwined with its people's lives that it's much more than just a place of work - everyone there is much more than just a colleague. Yes, that might sound like pure Cheddar, but the holidays, the births, the deaths, the weddings, the birthdays, the Christmasses, the anniversaries and the reunions are a type of social reinforcement way beyond employment. They are the stuff of kin.
MURRAY AITKEN, FORMER BRINKWORTH DIRECTOR

We do work really hard. Work hard, play hard, is absolutely underlining what we do but what differs here is that we are all treated as equals. When I started working with them both I really appreciated the relaxed way they both appeared for work. Kev would arrive in the office after already spending hours on site and a lap around Victoria Park with his dog Jackson, and Ad would rock up a little hot after skateboarding in one of his many Caps and Vans combos. 12 years on they are both still showing up for work in exactly the same way.
KAREN BYFORD, MANAGING DIRECTOR

It is a work culture that was commented on time and time again by staff, clients and collaborators during interviews, a generosity of spirit that runs right through the company. It is this generosity that allows the company to experiment and innovate with its work, as it does not stand still or take the easy way out of a project when a more challenging yet intellectually stimulating idea or project or possibility arises. Albeit one that might not be the most financially rewarding.

I would say that as a company, I think we're quite generous and quite honest with our clients. Adam is way too generous and way too honest. Quite often we're like, 'No, Adam, we're not doing it for free'. EMMA WYNN, DIRECTOR

It's a culture that can be deceptive. Whereas everyone looks like they are breezing through the working day, there is an underlying focus, an energy of intensity.

Deep down, it's a bit like an iceberg, it can be pretty intense. There's a perception that it's relaxed, chilled and we're all having a great time, but, underlying that, people work really hard. GRAHAM RUSSELL, ASSOCIATE DIRECTOR

In this culture of openness, a non-hierarchical structure where people are treated equally and openly, how have they been able to achieve such a high volume of work, yet still maintain that equality, whilst ensuring a curiosity and openness to experimentation, new ideas and challenges?

PROCESSES

We are not arrogant; we don't think we know the answers. We are actually really generous and kind and helpful to our customers, and we go out of our way to produce a good space for them. We really enjoy doing the same thing again, and again, and again. Because if you do it again, even in the same place, you can improve the mistakes and keep it innovative. ADAM BRINKWORTH

The seemingly simple linear approach to a project belies the complexities of each stage, as well as the time spent on each one. But it is fair to say the company prioritise a good dynamic between themselves and the client in order to see the whole of the project to fruition and completion.

I personally have two clear priorities - one is that the original concept is strong, relevant and imaginative, and second, that there is no escaping the truth in three dimensions as a finalized project. ADAM BRINKWORTH

Discovering and defining the parameters of the project help to formulate the brief and identify fundamental aspects such as the expectations of all parties involved in the process. Essentials, such as budget and the realistic outcomes for all parties involved in the collaboration, must be defined. Successful definition stages lead to a strong brief, practical budgets, sensible timelines and realistic expectations.

Design Concept stage is driven by creative responses to the brief. This will usually also involve the interrogation of the specifics of a site or location for the project. These factors reinvest new parameters into the design proposal. It is in this stage that materials might be introduced along with products, and their possible methods of display. Brinkworth's material obsessions often mean that they will introduce them wherever it is possible throughout the stages of the process.

We like to involve the client in the material pallet really early on, that can lead to a wealth of finishes. I think the work shows that, because there is always a profusion of materials in them. In turn, this attracts the clients. A Brinkworth project is always full of materials, it is never just a white box. KEVIN BRENNAN

In order to develop a scheme, the analysis of the planning and its resolution is of paramount importance. Objects such as furniture, clothes displays, reception desks and counters, as well as larger elements such as the arrangement of rooms and the planning of a user journey, will all be meticulously researched and then synthesised into plan, section, elevation and examined through three-dimensional representations such as a model.

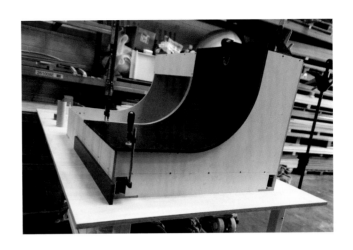

It's understanding the material, you know, the stuff that's available to allow you to do that. That's really important for me. It might be just a little sketch of a one to five of a doorframe but that could be the spirit of the whole project. That's what drives me. KEVIN BRENNAN

Developing the detail of the project will include the utilisation of knowledge on materiality and its maintenance, and detailed specifications on all aspects of the space. Only then can it be delivered successfully.

My obsession with details is because once someone realises that you know what you're talking about, you can have a much better creative journey with the people making your work. Rather than, 'I don't care but I want it to look like that.' It's all about detail. KEVIN BRENNAN

One of the last aspects of the project timeline is delivery. This requires a carefully selected contractor who can assemble the space with the appropriate level of care and quality. Delays in this part of the process, whilst sometimes unavoidable if dealing with a site where unexpected issues are found, will lead to financial penalties. For instance a delay of a week of opening a retail space will lead to approximately 20% of the build budget being added to the costs. This is obviously not a good situation.

Finally, activation is not just about the process but also the gauging of success. Post-occupation analysis is undertaken to ensure all aspects of the completed and delivered design are operating in the manner by which they were intended. This phase can also clear up any changes or additions, a fine-tuning moment to ensure the project is a success for all concerned.

The processes of a Brinkworth project are well defined and have been honed not just due to the numerous projects they have completed, but also as a result of their origins as manufacturer.

MATERIALITIES

My material, my pallet is Jewson's and a steel yard, it's nothing more than that. KEVIN BRENNAN

The early formative years defined the development of a rigorous strong work ethic. It was one that was forged in the white heat of four-week project turnovers: one week design, two weeks manufacturing, one week fitting. Resourcefulness on the design and fitting of the Karen Millen stores meant that the flat Adam was living in, his dad's small flat in South London, was rapidly being outgrown as a workshop, but it had not become totally defunct. One store design and build required the ingenious use of the entrance gateway.

So, there wasn't a budget to go and get the key clamp rolled, like a steel tube. At the time he was living in his dad's flat. It was like a Victorian terrace house with brick pillars, and a wrought iron gate at the front. He just used two brick pillars so could just bend it, and these were three-metre-long bits of scaffold tube. He was just tweaking them very carefully, to get his long, gentle curve.
MICHAEL MARRIOTT

Resourcefulness and contingency have remained a distinct part of the company's ethos. They have formed an enduring commitment to working with all kinds of materials, and have forged an approach that has ensured that the company has always had a very active response to the choosing and assemblage of materials. Thinking and then making has always been an intrinsic part of the processes of their design work.

The obsession with material, and honed into a process-driven understanding of the specifics of a project and its site, formed the unique blueprint for the company's future working processes. This attention to detail is important to all the staff.

What Brinkworth bring that other similar agencies in the field don't necessarily bring is that real attention to detail. We look to go from the macro to the micro and so you'll get something that looks good from a distance but looks great close up, and in five years' time still looks great close up because it's been made with appropriate materials and appropriate detailing. SONNY CANT, DIRECTOR

This approach also extends to the site:

We approach our work architecturally, asking ourselves what can this amazing space, its volume and core materiality lend to our scheme. Once we have that we can suitably layer our ideas in. KAREN BYFORD, MANAGING DIRECTOR

The site specificity of the work Brinkworth does means that each venture has the capacity to be a unique fusion of place and project.

It's the memories you can get from an experience in a space. What people can take away from . . . it has to be a unique experience in order to ensure it endures and impacts upon the user. KAREN BYFORD

COLLABORATORS AND CULTURE

COLLABORATORS

The reality is, with Kevin and with Adam, I think they feel their projects. As a client, I think you want your consultants to feel their work; to intuitively understand it, and not to roll things out by numbers. They take on projects that they like, which is very, very rare. They're the first to tell me, 'Look, you're wrong, Rog.' They often say it in a lot stronger words than that... ROGER WADE, BOXPARK

Collaboration between the practice and their clients ensures that each phase of the process in a project undergoes a dynamic challenge: one that focuses on the stretching of any initial preconceptions of the design work and tests thoroughly what both parties may want from the process.

The thing about Brinkworth I've always liked is that it's less corporate, it's less high street, even though they've got lots of high street customers. They're not trying too hard. They're also not egocentric. I don't think it's about their view of the world and leading the customer through their view of the world. SIMON MOTTRAM, RAPHA

The challenges and risks of this way of working have meant that particular clients return, often repeatedly: they are invigorated by the encounter. The process has not only produced an interesting space, the journey to get there has challenged their own working practices. Because of this, many enduring friendships have been formed, many of which have evolved with the practice.

I would struggle to find a negative thing to say about Adam, he's an incredibly generous guy, I mean meticulously so. It's part of the Brinkworth identity, there's a generosity, how much they give to people, time, thought, gifts. And I think if you're a client, that's the way you receive the work, they have gifted me with this idea. I think that's a real part of the identity. Kevin is like the sort of mountain of that place. It's a bad analogy because he's such a rounded super-interesting guy. The work he does is remarkable. I cannot think highly enough of the guy. He can do anything. ADRIAN CADDY, GREENSPACE

The results of this mixture of resourcefulness, innovation, energy, attention to detail are the processes of utilising what is available and getting the best from it. In challenging themselves to produce something more than a conventional design has meant that the 2500 projects that they have completed are all an advanced synthesis of their learning and experience at that given time. All of them are bespoke,

I honestly don't think we would have built Karen Millen with anyone else. I mean we had something very special together and I'm not sure I could have found anyone else who would put up with me actually.
KEVIN STANFORD ON WORKING WITH ADAM BRINKWORTH

As well as their origins, the other critical factors in the formation and subsequently the culture of the practice are the associations they form with their clients and the relationships they have with the employees of the company. Brinkworth have always attracted exacting clients, people who require that the designers not only meet their requirements but, in that process, will challenge them, will make them rethink their needs and (sometimes forcefully) inform the client when they are not matching the practice's level of input. Yet calling them clients feels impersonal and lacks connection. Friends is too comfortable a term, yet this is what many clients become. However a project works out, working with Brinkworth, for both friends and the practice, is not always an effortless procedure. Both collaborators, clients and the practice will challenge the assumptions of all participants in order to achieve the best results.

site-specific responses to a place, a set of situations, client requirements, financial demands and numerous constraints. What drives them to deliver this high quality production line of bespoke, customised, provocative set of spaces for a set of informed and exacting clients, as if anew each time?

They have all the usual accolades of peer admiration and awards, lots of them but, whilst enjoyable, these are not their motivation. What drives them on is fascination and the challenge to produce places that innovate and to make something new that does not just fit their client's needs but reconfigures any thoughts of them. They are fired by the intelligence of design thinking, the responsiveness to new challenges and an enduring curiosity to adapt and produce exceptional work.

Brinkworth are a set of interesting people, doing exciting work in an environment that is very generous and spirited. Words that come to mind are co-operative, collaborative, with an attitude and vision in an environment of continual learning. It is a location in which to flourish and there is a lot of love in the room. PAT MEAGHER, CONSULTANT

This ethos of the company is derived from a fusion of the two partners and their team and their approach to design work. It is a distinct, down-to-earth work ethic. It is one that is coupled with a strong material sensibility. It is a methodology that directs not only how they make space but also how their company operates, how it values its friends, clients, colleagues, peers. It is the result of years of experience, forged through a deep understanding of making, an innate comprehension of materiality, fused with a desire to think things through and challenge the users of their spaces to experience something new. Fundamentally Adam and Kevin's respect for each other and their different approaches not only formulates the practice's dynamic, it keeps them working together.

Adam's passionate enthusiasm rubs off on the people around him. He inspires both the team and the clients with his steadfast love of what he does.
LOUISE MELCHIOR, PR DIRECTOR, PHOTOGRAPHER

CULTURE

If Brinkworth was a band then it's one that is constantly changing and looking for new material. It is a band that creates and strives for that new sound, that delivers something which stimulates the senses, a sound that wants to be different, better and fresher than the last. A band that through practice, crafts its sound, matures and moves on to greater things. A band that lets other band members have a voice, try something out, inspire and add creative input for the greater good of the result. A band that is serious about what it does but above all enjoys the ride to the gigs. RICHARD BLURTON, FORMER BRINKWORTH DESIGNER

Anybody who has worked in a creative practice will be able to relay numerous stories of the parties, friendship-forming late-night working, mishaps, mistakes, projects and the working practices of a place. Some of these stories and some of those practices have become more legendary and more notorious than others, but the real culture of a creative practice is not always something that is so straightforward to discern. The signifiers of the unique culture of a practice can be gleaned from many places. Not least their own studio, but also the spaces they inhabit outside of work.

Since 1900 Pellicci's café has been serving food to the locals on Bethnal Green Road. It has been an integral part of Brinkworth's culture since Adam took over the studio in 1993 and for the last 20 years has not just been a place to eat, but has also been the location of their infamous Christmas parties. On these occasions, they take over the café.

A long time ago I asked Tony what was the capacity of the café and I thought he said 43. Our policy for years was to never employ more than 43 people, but I heard him wrong and it was actually 34. ADAM BRINKWORTH

It was not until 2017 that the café capacity could not hold all of the staff team, and so they organised a one-off pop-out, where the café was expanded for a very short period of time to take all of the staff in one sitting for the party.

You can go anywhere you want, I know how you treat your lot, you travel, you can go to the best hotels and restaurants in the world, but you love coming here. It's great for us. NEV PELLICCI

The café is just one aspect of the culture of the company and part of the atmosphere and approach to the wellbeing of staff in the practice. The studio space, the café, the local pubs are all extensions of the Brinkworth culture, as the studio is fully integrated into its local context.

The social aspect to any business is important to get right. Social practices work well together and generate the right atmosphere. Brinkworth place great emphasis on this.

I like to think that people who have worked here over the years have had a good working experience, but I know they have had a good social one. These go deeply together so everyone can see that this is what we are doing, this is how we do it. ADAM BRINKWORTH

Small things such as birthdays are always remembered and celebrated, big things such as memorable moments in the practice's history are honoured, and are celebrated lavishly. The recent 25th-birthday celebration exemplified the esteem in which the company is regarded and the warmth the company feels for its staff, clients, colleagues, collaborators, family and friends. Renting the Oval Space in Hackney, close to a thousand guests danced the night away to Norman Jay and Rice Cube, with food and drink supplied by clients Ollie Dabbous and Oskar Kinberg. Even practice leavers exit in style:

On my final leaving day I arrived at the studio to find it strangely quiet. Upon approaching my desk all of the Brinkworth staff at the time rose from behind the table in the meeting room, all donned in Derby County football shirts. I can say the team have never looked so good as that day … that's Brinkworth. RICHARD BLURTON

As well as the Bethnal Green context, the studio itself is a signifier of the working practices of the company and by extension a projection of their culture.

I love the location where they are. It probably sums it all up, it's unassuming, it's cool. It is egalitarian and there is an enthusiastic workforce. That's all to do with the DNA of Adam himself, he wants people to be treated as he wanted to be treated in the past. It represents his characteristics. Everyone's passionate and these are essential qualities that embody a successful business. I don't see any hierarchy there, great ideas come first. If you've got a great idea, put it on the table. PAN PHILIPPOU, DIESEL, BEN SHERMAN

It's not po-faced and overly serious. It always felt like that, and I like that very much. As I say, there were bikes everywhere, down in the kitchen inside, and stuff.
SIMON MOTTRAM, RAPHA

As creative people the staff are drawn to the atmosphere of the building and the people in it:

I liked the multi-disciplinary background of the staff – furniture, product design, etc. – and the hands-on approach. I liked the idea that Brinkworth built things. I also liked the fact that the entrance to the studio was through a small door set inside a larger set of doors and that initially I had to share my desk with Floyd, Kev's dog. He had dibs on the space underneath as he was there first.
HOWARD SMITH, PRACTICE DIRECTOR

The non-hierarchical organisation of the office really spells out how the company likes to portray its values to clients. It's an atmosphere of openness. It's a welcoming spirit that enthuses clients and collaborators who visit or work with them in Bethnal Green:

I go down and see the team in Bethnal Green and it's not, 'I am …' it's, 'We are …' It really is so important.
PAN PHILIPPOU

The prevailing culture of the Brinkworth studio creates an atmosphere of trust, a sense that things are possible because risk taking is admired. A certain chutzpah is required to thrive in an office like Brinkworth, but it's a characteristic that is fully supported and encouraged as it leads to a natural ease with which to allow creativity to come to the fore:

They work very hard at making it like a family, but in a very natural way. They want everyone to be happy because that's absolutely just their nature. I think there is a thing which perhaps comes out of the in-house spirit, which is a sort of braveness, and a kind of attitude that's like, 'Well, let's fucking try it.' MICHAEL MARRIOTT

The introduction to this culture can be a little daunting:

When I first started, I thought it was one of the craziest places that I'd been in. In my first two weeks, I had to organise a bar crawl. I got insanely drunk. We went away for an accountant's 50th to Dublin. I was also blown away with how warm everyone was, and friendly, which is normally a perception that you don't think you'll have. Because I'd come in, and there were all these trendy, slick designers. You've got Adam, who's basically Santa Claus, and a yes man, and is just doing anything to make sure people are having a good time, and put a smile on their faces. The people work really, really hard, but play really hard too. BEN ASSEFA-FOLIVI, STUDIO MANAGER

But it's a culture that allows its people to excel and really find their feet. Staff stay at Brinkworth; and those that do leave often choose come back as they cannot find that experience or unique culture in other places.

It's very much a family I would say. I think because it was so small for so long it's kind of kept that. I think the staff like being able to see things like progress, for instance having somebody like me who's gone from work experience to a director is quite a positive thing.
SONNY CANT, DIRECTOR

I really feel like I've found the place that I was looking to work at because what they have allowed me to do is to have the autonomy in design that I was always searching for.
EMMA WYNN, DIRECTOR

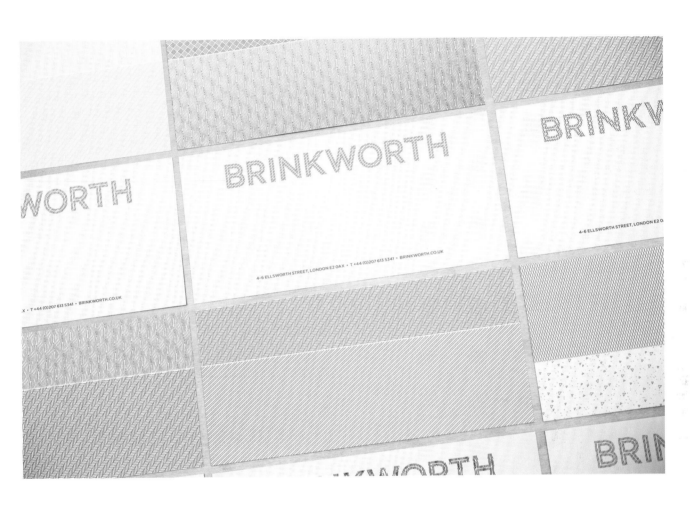

In 2014 Brinkworth commissioned Graphic Thought Facility, to redesign the company branding. The logo itself is a clean, simple sans serif word mark that can be inset into a variety of custom-drawn patterns based on architectural cross-hatching.

above: Michael Marriott
top right and middle: Carl Clerkin
bottom: Fiona Banner

opposite, top: Ben Kelly
bottom left: Konstantin Grcic
bottom right: Gavin Turk

Beyond the legendary stories and parties, how work is undertaken and the atmosphere of the place, tell-tale signs of a culture can be found in how a practice will support and develop its staff. Brinkworth are committed to its people and the support of their work and education. The annual trips of the practice to Venice, and other European cities of culture and the regular invites to talk at universities, professional events, externally examine, teach, write reviews, as well as inviting people to talk in the practice (Fiona Banner, Carl Turner, Gavin Turk, Konstantin Grcic, Benedict Radcliffe), demonstrate a willingness to maintain curiosity and keep learning as a central component of the life and culture of the practice. As Kevin Brennan summed up:

We still want the studio to be a bit like an art college really.

Many interviewees mentioned the warmth of the company, its generosity, it's a spirit that prevails, but it's one that comes with a sense of focus, an industriousness, but also with a restlessness that is an impatience to carry on making things better, and better again. This is the Brinkworth culture. Hard working and focused but with a creative dynamic that is realised socially, as well as through their practice and their work.

PLACES

Amongst the numerous spaces completed by Brinkworth, there are a number of projects that stand out as benchmarks in the company's evolution. These are spaces where a particular synthesis of client, space, site, design, process, materiality, budget have all coalesced to provide a dynamic realisation of an interior. New ground has been broken. This chapter examines these projects in depth. They have been organised under the three headings of Places, Identities and Communities: three elements that the company has relentlessly explored throughout so much of its work.

PLACES

In the conventional world of contemporary interior design, and in particular in retail design, the instinct to create spaces that can be modularised and rolled-out is pervasive. This creates a tension in the design of the interior where the particulars of a site and the requirements of a client will often all mitigate against the desire for repetition: the focus is to produce a unique experience that is found in an exceptional environment. Designers of interior space often want to create environments that are at best an impressive event. At the very least some form of significant impression should be left on the occupant. In retail environments it is often the case that the brand experience may result in some form of allegiance and maybe even the consumption of some form of a product. Whichever way the design of an interior space is considered, the creation of a distinct place is important. It is critical that the experience can be leveraged through a particular site and will be extracted and mined for its full potential. It is the proximity and the distribution of elements in a particular place that form some kind of significance, it is a distinct character or quality that makes a particular place and therefore forms a distinct kind of experience.

An understanding of place can also extend to acknowledging that it's just a backdrop for the activities that are about to take place there. Much has been written about the pop-up or guerrilla approach – a short, sharp temporal object, space, intervention that can be used as an instrument to generate interest in a brand or company. When this approach is utilised place becomes part of the narrative, and the more interesting a place, the better the story. When Brinkworth developed an intervention into Dover Street Market in London for Stutterheim, they counterpointed the colourful Swedish raincoats with their placement in an off-the-peg lean-to shack, constructed with corrugated tin roofing and a simple shed-like timber frame. The blackened structure appeared ramshackle and in stark contrast to the shiny crafted apparel. A nod to Swedish-noir films and melancholia, the contrast between the colourful objects and their monochromatic context provided a powerful image, one that impressed a short sharp shock upon the visual senses of the visitor to the space.

Making place is not just confined to responding to an existing building. The use of a unique environment to create a distinct experience can extend to the selection of an inimitable landscape. UVU, a maker of specialist technical apparel for running in extreme climates, required a space that could tell the story of the product, its concept, as well as attract possible retail partners. Working with Fresh Britain, the first stage of this process took the form of evolving an environment with which to generate interest. Because of its association with the great outdoors, the National Geographic Society in London was chosen to house the first stage of the story telling. A temporary pop-up structure was designed and installed in the society's Georgian room. Standing independently of the room the environments extracted the maximum theatricality, from the tension between the ornate and well-proportioned room and the new temporary elements.

In order to expand the narrative of the product and brand, the next stage was to design a pop-up at the North Pole, in the form of a marathon finishing line. The fact that this inhospitable environment would attract no customer footfall was not important. Instead, the image of the object in the environment was critical as the simple tent structure was positioned amongst the vast expanse of ice. Inside the tent products were displayed on ice, demonstrating their performance in extreme environments and temperatures. Ultimately, the white tent, with numerous colourful flags surrounding it, became a symbol for the company: a brand image of startling simplicity and utter effectiveness.

The distinct culture of the making of place through the work of Brinkworth has resulted in many exceptional interior spaces. Whether a residential, work, shop or play space, the practice has endeavoured to create uniquely configured combinations of site and space in order to impress a unique experience on the participants.

This chapter shows a number of projects that foreground ideas of place-making in the design process and outcomes. They are projects that emphasise the coexistence of numerous elements in order to make a distinct spatial experience.

ALLSAINTS

Launched in 1995, Brinkworth were invited to design the clothing brand's stand-alone retail space in central London. They knew that the brand needed an instantly recognisable presence on the street. They also wanted to create an interior that redefined the relationship between the garment and the enclosure in which it was displayed. How could the new space strengthen the brand identity and make it instantly recognisable?

The iconography of the cross intrigued us, but due to its religious significance, it wouldn't work in all markets. We liked the fairground imagery of the light bulbs with which to make a statement. We chose to emphasise the sewing machines upfront as we were interested in multiples and how they created impact, and how they connected the brand to the rag trade and the manufacturing history of Spitalfields. KEVIN BRENNAN

The presence on the street was conveyed through what appeared to be a counter-intuitive strategy. Conventional retail interior wisdom, where precious window display is used to lure customers inside the shop, was turned on its head. Instead of a clear, unfettered view, the shop window became a powerful abstract signifier that projected the processes of making the clothing - a facade that required the viewer to work a little in order to understand and be curious as to what lay beyond it. Filling the store window,

and partially obscuring the view into the interior, were hundreds of second-hand Singer sewing machines. Each was placed upon a key-clamp steel frame. (In later stores this idea was extended to the interior, and wall upon wall of sewing machines would snake through the inside space, often starting at the entrance to the store, and leading the customer deep into the space.) In essence the machines were fetishised and displayed as though in vitrines in a dusty old museum. Whether a comment on the production processes of garment making, or just marvelling at the old machinery of a rag trade gone by, the display set the scene for the interior inside.

Exposed steel structures, stripped back brickwork, cracked plaster, roughly-hewn timber walls and floors meant that the decay of the interior counterpointed the artfully managed rawness of the garments. These raw edges and exposed surfaces and seams personified a close connection to the processes of the fabrication of ALLSAINTS' clothing. A found approach to each site, exemplified through the exposed surfaces of the existing building, the raw space, and the subsequent installation of the iconic vintage sewing machine, meant that none of the ALLSAINTS' spaces would ever be the same. Whatever was found on site would be either incorporated into the exiting store or edited out. And if the context was not interesting enough, new elements would be added to give it character.

The theatre of the interior was advanced with stage-set and gantry lighting, along with the ALLSAINTS' cross logo or name picked out in bulb-lighting inspired by seeing the lights on Brighton's seafront and the Palace Pier. The theatricality of the interior was exemplified in the dark, moody, atmospheric interiors of the space. In later stores the Gothic overtones would be re-emphasised with black-mirrored glass and Corten steel. If possible the facades of shops would also be clad in steel, embellished with the postcode coordinates of the ALLSAINTS' brand in Spitalfields, East London, in order to intensify the shock of a window of old garment making machinery stacked up in a space.

The instant success of this carefully considered, intelligent and economic imagery meant that the identity of the brand was consolidated. Cleverly, the potential for a roll-out identikit, a modularised generic format, was avoided through the notion that each space was an opportunity to extract and strip back the story of the place through the removal of its years' accretions. This approach was re-emphasised by the vintage sewing machine, a symbolic reminder of the past of garment production, thus ensuring that each space would always be a distinctive, original place, one that was mixed with the familiarity of the iconic machine, a relic from the past, alongside the new, distinctive clothing of the company.

KENT RESERVOIR

The experience of going into this old reservoir was quite amazing. It didn't feel anything like a living space, so for Kevin to see the potential in it, that was the genius behind the project. DINOS CHAPMAN

A decommissioned 1930s concrete structure, designed to house 500,000 gallons of water in a reservoir, was remodelled to make a five-bedroom house for the artist Dinos Chapman and fashion designer Tiphaine De Lussy. The 7,500-square-foot building was originally encased in 'bunds' of earth that took the weight of the water and ensured it was structurally sound. Upon seeing the building in its dilapidated state, the monumental scale and the melancholic ambience of the abandoned structure reinforced the design strategy: an approach that ensured that its reuse would be based around what was already there. This tactic would ensure that the new design would work with the existing building and yet assert its compliance yet autonomy from the concrete-grid structure, thereby creating a unique house, a one-off place to call a home.

The early preparation works for the project involved stripping back the building to reveal its outline, clarifying the existing site much like an archaeological dig. The earthworks that surrounded the building were excavated in order to expose the magnificence of the monumental building. It was clear that the internal logic of the structure of the grid of the concrete building would provide the basic formal system from which the new plan would emerge. Therefore the simplicity of the new domestic space meant that the reservoir structure would, with carefully considered cut-out glazed openings placed into the walls of the building, contain the bedrooms and the living room, as well as kitchen and dining area. On top of the structure would be a new Mies-like glass and steel pavilion, set inside the footprint of the building, which would contain a living space with views across the north downs of Kent. Its black painted structure and ceiling was designed to make it disappear into the night sky. A steel staircase from the lower level of the space would access this elevated room, surrounded by glass and yet with the furniture sunk into a timber floor. The recessed furniture was designed to avoid any confusion with the ridge of the downs in the distance. The sunken space could afford its occupants a panoramic view of the sky, framed by the floor to ceiling glazing, and the black steel parapet. The effect was intended to enact a James Turrell skyspace experience: outlining a carefully delineated view of a combined landscape and sky.

A long strip of roof was removed in order to create a walled courtyard. An 80-foot lap pool was designed to span the whole length of the sunken courtyard in the lower floor: reflecting natural light down and into the five bedrooms that were lined up alongside it. It was accessed from each space through full length glass doors. Whilst providing the inhabitants of the house with an elaborate exercise and play space, the long thin tank of water encapsulated a direct connection to the past water retaining function of the reservoir building. Its 'weir-edge' engineered wet wall being a constant reminder of the movement of water, the building's very reason for being.

The relentless logic of the concrete shell ensured that the interior could essentially be designed to respond in two ways: it could either be distributed in and around the exposed columns, steering free of the structure, or be aligned to absorb the organising frame. As well as its determinant impact on the distribution of the interior space, the materiality of the frame and existing building was utilised in order to maintain a constant and sometimes unambiguous reminder of the previous life of the space. New materials matched the robust surface conditions of the structure. A polished concrete floor and black brick with grey pointing was offset with warmer oak panelling in the living rooms of the lower level. Bedrooms were finished in white render walls that offset the stark grain of the aggregate of the bare concrete soffit. The upper level pavilion floor was sunken into a tray of oak flooring.

The previous function of the building and its brooding introspective intensity was transformed into a welcoming family home. The house provided a haven for the family and allowed them to escape from the distractions of the city. Yet its heavy intensity, its unrelenting structure and significant connection to its previous use ensured that it provoked strong feelings from its new owners.

It was a testament to the capacity and vision of the designers that recognised the potential of the building to be transformed into a family home: a place that recognised its past and yet had been reprogrammed for a new future.

GREENSPACE

Through the co-existence of a configuration of objects, a place can be formed through the combination of things that then form their narrative. This suggests that the formation of a series of elements are the things that promote and form this resonance. This vibrant matter is stable, an implication of a legacy, and a suggestion that implies that a space can be made into a place that resonates for its inhabitants for a significant period of time.

After working at Imagination for a number of years, whilst setting up his own practice Adrian Caddy was approached by Heineken to undertake some research into their core audience. Instead of taking a conventional route, Caddy was interested in how this research might be approached in a new way. He wanted to understand what Heineken's audience was into, how they lived their lives, what their tastes were, their interests and so on. In particular Heineken were interested in the idea of exchange, how their product can facilitate connection, even if just a simple 'cheers' between two people.

Adrian Caddy was aware of how brand research, at the time, was exploring how changes were evolving particular relationships between product and user, and how companies were starting to explore how the customer could participate in a fuller, more engaged experience of a brand. Companies were exploring how participants could co-create their experience and make it more bespoke and connected. This would be a form of participation that meant that users had a central role in the product they were experiencing through the co-creation, or collaboration, of the production of the narrative or message of the brand. As well as this, Caddy was aware that the normal approach to attaching a logo to a sport event or music festival was no longer enough in order to fully engage brand users. Based on these responses, Caddy developed Greenspace.

I had an idea called 'Greenspace'. Heineken is green, and the concept of that mind-set that you go to when you meet someone. It's a metaphor for what Heineken's all about. Creating a place or a mental space where people can fill with their own experiences, co-create a festival, one that could travel around.
ADRIAN CADDY, FOUNDER AND DIRECTOR OF GREENSPACE

Greenspace was a place where people could create their own experience, a festival where the participants curated the content. Its title was partially related to the green brand colour of Heineken, but also related to ideas of parklands and places where participants were invited to adopt a different mind-set than they would have in the city. Caddy's idea was instantly liked by the brand, and it was then that he thought of Brinkworth as a company who could help him evolve and realise the idea spatially. Caddy was aware of Brinkworth's work and he considered that they shared a similar sensibility and approach. He knew he wanted a company that was not too mannered and formal, and who could approach the project in an open-minded yet challenging way.

Greenspace started its initial journey in 2002 and was realised in 2005 in Valencia, Spain. Valencia was chosen due to various other activities going on in the city at that time, such as the America's Cup (2007) as well as hosting its third art biennale. More importantly was the negotiation and subsequent acquisition of a space in which to launch the five-year sponsored venue; a series of large, open abandoned warehouses just south of the city centre. The warehouses were originally grain stores, and then had been used as a travellers' camping ground. They were in significant disrepair. The project would kick-start the subsequent renovation: in 2010 it became a fully remodelled cultural venue, as well as a place for start-ups and new creative entrepreneurs.

Caddy initiated and developed an idea around the use of an off-the-peg element: the shipping container. Inspired by the fact that Heineken were one of the worlds biggest users of containers, and thus they were iconic to the brand, and realising that the event space would need to be temporary, Caddy also realised that anything placed into the cavernous warehouse interiors would need to have a spatial presence. He invited Brinkworth to further develop the idea. They were offered Heineken containers but Brinkworth's manufacturing experience ensured that they knew these would not withstand recycling. Instead they designed and built their own. These became a series of six containerised spaces. They housed exhibition spaces and bars, some of which had the capacity to be stacked to form a changeable landscape of spaces, and be set up in various configurations for numerous events.

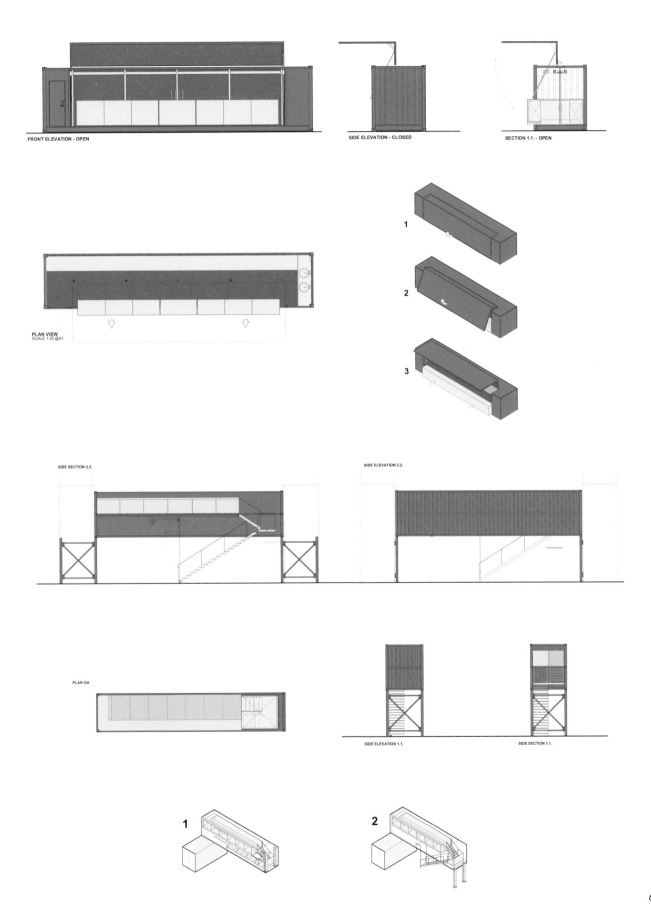

FRONT ELEVATION - OPEN

SIDE ELEVATION - CLOSED

SECTION 1.1. - OPEN

PLAN VIEW
SCALE 1:25 @A1

1

2

3

SIDE SECTION 2.2.

SIDE ELEVATION 2.2.

PLAN GA

SIDE ELEVATION 1.1.

SIDE SECTION 1.1.

1

2

The containers were custom-made in Liverpool by the workshops that had previously fabricated all of the stainless-steel work for Karen Millen. They were shipped to the site where they were forklifted into position. The final fit-out was continued on site. The series of bar containers were reworked so that either a single or both sides could be hydraulically raised to open up for business. Like gull-wings, as each panel lifted it revealed a full-length shiny steel bar. The sides of another container were split to open out to extend its exhibition walls. The ready-made qualities of the containers was completed with graphics, added by local sign-makers and with other graphics stencilled on the side.

After holding over 400 events over six years, the space was sold to a developer. The legacy of the project was that in the three warehouse spaces there is now a 1,500-seat theatre and an adjacent more flexible performance space, along with a number of studio spaces for start-up companies. Greenspace kick-started a unique combination of brand development and leveraging the co-creation of unique experiences, as well as the significant development of a part of the city. This left a legacy of development that will assist in the city's creative future, as the project aroused the interest of designers and architects as a potential new model for city development:

This, in my eyes, shows that there is perhaps a new moment where corporations are, or want to be seen to be, generous or unilateral. The whole Greenspace project has been defined in a very clever way.
REM KOOLHAAS, ARCHITECT OMA

LBi

Inspired by early spatial memories of his experiences when visiting his father's workplace in a Gillette razor factory in Reading, and nights spent in the cavernous interior spaces of the Hacienda nightclub in Manchester, Kevin Brennan was very keen to undertake the LBi project when they approached Brinkworth to design their new London headquarters. The project was to reconfigure a huge warehouse, just off Brick Lane and part of the extensive estate of the Truman Brewery, in order to house the 500-strong staff of the company. Just like the factories that Brennan was influenced by, the project gave Brinkworth the opportunity to explore the reworking of a powerful industrial relic, and the chance to make a unique place that would radically transform not just the building but also the surrounding area as its workers colonised the new headquarters.

Known as the old Keg-store, the 60,000-square-foot brick and steel frame building was initially designed for the production and storage of beer in the brewing process. Therefore the ingress of natural light was not considered important or useful when it was constructed. This needed to change in its adaptation for a workspace, where light and view would be critically important.

In order to let natural light into the interior Brinkworth opened up the north elevation of the building and filled it with a series of Reglit glass planks. Part of the ground floor was also removed. These structural changes allowed light to pour into the interior space and into the basement, ensuring it could be used as an event space. As well as the new glass wall signalling the entrance to the design studios, a long steel-clad ramp ascended from street level to the front door. The vast scale of the interior space, and the robust structure of the existing building, meant that new structural loadings could easily be accommodated on the columns and beams of the building. Two new mezzanines were hung from the structure, creating more intimate workspaces, spatial variation in the interior, and ensuring that the existing ground and first floors were not cluttered with new columns.

A robust, industrial-strength palette of material finishes of steel, glass, polished concrete and wooden floors evolved and completed the factory aesthetic of the existing building. The markings of a basketball court where added to the basement in order to give the floor scale and emphasize the size of the space. Combined together, the aesthetic was of a tough industrial space that was asking its new inhabitants to make it their own workplace and construct a new chapter in the building's history.

I think that the LBi project was a key one for us. That was me coming out of the shadows and it was an important project for me. It's a big industrial space brewery, and I have always been attracted to factory spaces. It really blew me away and I was fascinated by the raw space. KEVIN BRENNAN

Kevin's ability to see the potential in a space, rip it apart in order to maximise light, space and function is incredible. LOUISE MELCHIOR, PR DIRECTOR, PHOTOGRAPHER

NETHERHALL GARDENS

What comes across strongly at No 48, is the materiality, object-quality and spatial quirks. The entrance facade - mainly black, dark grey-pointed brick, glass, with two big openings at first and second floor levels at the north-east corner - is foreign to the streetscape; yet the building's position on the site, the height of its flat, truncated ridge, and the treatment of the east elevation . . . has produced a composition whose graphic outline clarity and matt, monochromatic regression is intriguingly civil.
JAY MERRICK, *ARCHITECTURAL REVIEW*, JUNE 2017

The first domestic new-build completed by the practice replaced an existing post-war semi-detached house on a site in Hampstead, North London. Described as an essay in the reworking of the suburban semi-detached typology, the house is far more sophisticated and spatially complex than its predecessor. The result of its difficult location, and the accompanying building regulations, the house is a taut assemblage of rooms wrapped in considered material form.

Designing a family home is never a straightforward affair. It is a complicated project, one where the essential requirements of life are combined with the aspirations and hopes of clients. These are then coerced into a set of responses that are compelled to interrogate the pragmatics of place, site, regulations and budget. This house is all of these things and more. It is a subtle weave of form and structural tension, articulating the desires of the family and the challenge of a very particular site, with a very specific set of constraints.

On approach, through its arrangement of bays, windows and front door, the atypical, solid semi-detached house would normally present itself face-on to the street: inviting its visitor to immediately and assuredly recognise its inner spatial distribution. Whilst deriving its origins from the typical semi-detached, upon arrival, this house presents to the street what appears to be a gable end: a suggestion of a turned corner or edge. This introverted welcome is reinforced by the sharp geometry of the gable corner, where at the ground floor, a steel beam slides out of the masonry skin and extends away from the garden wall. It's a sophisticated move that whilst extending the ground floor kitchen space and allowing the covering of the basement stair in a glazed roof, flooding the basement in bright light, re-emphasises the frontal presentation of what is normally considered the side of a building. It's a masterful composition of formal dynamics, rendering a usually static or overlooked elevation, at the forefront of the entrance, by placing it front of house. Reinforcing the complexities of this usually reticent projection, the 'gable facade' is

punctuated by a large opening, stuck out of the brick. It's a mixed message. It is an open invitation to move through the house to the visible garden beyond, yet also presenting a side-on view: a cautious welcome to the entering guest.

Other formal tricks proliferate. Brennan conceived the building as though a brick box held up on exposed steels that span between two gardens walls. In turn the brick-faced two-storey upper structure is separated from the ground floor by a mostly glazed ground floor skin. This clear distinction of the upper and lower levels ensured that the building is read as though it is hovering atop the deep basement: itself a recess excavated to within half a metre of the local water table. This indicates the formation of a plinth base for the house, although one that is subtracted rather than added to the composition. The three storeys above the basement living room, contain the kitchen and dining room on the ground floor, and three bedrooms and bathrooms on the first floor and a master bedroom with en-suite on the second floor.

Each of the rooms on the first and second floors have unorthodox relationships with the brick box surrounding them. The front room on the first floor has a floor-to-ceiling corner opening facing back into the street. Set inside the main brick sidewall, it provides a small slither of external courtyard, a space that carefully modulates the views to the outside of the second floor. The corner of the master bedroom is incised into the room, making an external courtyard within the truncated-ridge gable end front wall of the house. The small external courtyard is an ambiguous space in that it is considered like another room in the house, yet it is outside. With its controlled views out of and into the house and its surroundings, a glazed floor, covering the void to a courtyard-like space at the rear of the building below, is a bridge to the terrace that takes you too a small garden. This detail renders the occupant unstable when they stand on the glass. It encapsulates the compacted tension of the manner by which the house is viewed, by both its inhabitants and by its neighbours.

The play and also the tension of the relationship between interior and exterior spaces within the rooms is palpable and enforces a close and intimate connection to the street on one side and the garden on the other. The house is a careful and skilful manipulation of both inside and outside spaces, representing the differing cadences of both private and public spaces, the essential components of any contemporary domestic place.

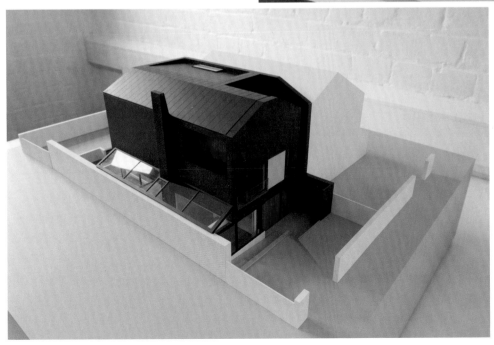

IDENTITIES

Brinkworth are the experts in the construction of very particular material identities. Their projects will often begin with an in-depth analysis of both the existing materials of a site and the new elements that may be included. It is not uncommon for an initial client meeting to take place around a table laden with samples of tile, steel, timber, images of surfaces and chunks of assembled materials: a process that avoids the clichés of the delicately assembled mood board, the currency of many interior offices.

It is an approach that could be considered counter-intuitive to the normal perceptions of the design process, where the concept or site might be thought of as the starting point of a project. Brinkworth consider that discussion of particular identities for interior space is often hugely reliant on the materials and surfaces chosen to represent space to its user. Different materials and how they are applied to space signify hugely different things to different types of people. Therefore, in the right hands, specific identities can be formed by the careful selection of very particular materials.

A project about the qualities of wood flooring exemplified the importance of the synthesis of space and materials to Brinkworth's working practices. Havwoods are a timber-floor specialist. Brinkworth created their London, New York and Berlin showrooms by exploring how they could exemplify the character and quality of the wooden flooring ranges, whilst allowing customers to experiment and explore different combinations of flooring. Instead of a traditional wall-based approach, the flooring samples were placed on table-tops, set flush within steel frames. Brushed brass draws underneath the displays can be opened to reveal more samples. They are reminiscent of large chest tables. In the London showroom this subtle and refined pallet of

Materiality is very important in all of our schemes and an almost obsessive attention to detail. There is always a consideration to engineering and production without being over the top or certainly trying to stay away from gimmicks or fads. Simple, well-constructed spaces is a good way of summing up what the office produces as a whole. SAM DERRICK, DIRECTOR

My time there taught me amongst other things, the importance of materiality, detail and a singular idea (or punchline, if Ad or Kev didn't get it, it wasn't worth getting). These attributes can be found in any Brinkworth project because fundamentally they underpin good design. MURRAY AITKEN, FORMER BRINKWORTH DIRECTOR

materials was used to discreetly enhance the range of flooring. It was extended to the stair that linked the upper and lower levels of the new showroom, creating a continuous material-based aesthetic for the space and hence the company. This material language was extended when the interior of a London Routemaster bus was transformed utilising the same pallet of materials to become a mobile showroom for the brand.

The combination of unusual materials is an approach that can ensure a memorable spatial resonance. END. the clothing brand commissioned Brinkworth to design their store in Glasgow in an old post-office building. The long thin space created circulation challenges that Brinkworth, which was overcome with the utilisation of a striking assemblage of materials. The length of the space was elongated with mirrored walls. Set against these surfaces was a lining of Calacatta Carrara marble, a beautiful white and grey veined stone. Juxtaposed with neon lights and bold END. graphics, the store's collections of clothes and shoes were repeated endlessly in the shimmering shiny surfaces of the mirrors and stone.

Throughout all of Brinkworth's projects careful attention to the material qualities is of paramount importance, and central to all stages of the project's journey.

BEN SHERMAN

Retail is theatre and it creates theatre. It was so important to get the shirt right. It was Brinkworth, trying to portray our new tone of voice, that was premium. It represented the new era of Ben Sherman. PAN PHILIPPOU, BEN SHERMAN

The theatrical aspect of retail spaces can be extended to the idea that the narrative projected by the objects and elements in a space can provide a unique link. This association is not just about the new stories being portrayed but it is also about forging a strong connection to the past, particularly if a space, a place or a brand has a well-established heritage. This is then a process of the forging of a link that reinforces the successful telling of stories and the evocation of empathy and connection; not only the fundamentals for the success of a stage presentation, but also for the creation of successful interior space.

Ben Sherman has a long and illustrious past but it was one that had become almost too synonymous with particular social movements; a situation that therefore had stymied any opportunity of it appealing to customers beyond this perceived clientele. This situation had extended to a failed attempt at launching a womenswear version of the brand. The failure was simple. Ben Sherman was just too closely associated with very particular, male-orientated, historic subcultures.

We worked to try to reposition the brand, it was very much in a cul-de-sac. If you didn't like the mods and you didn't like The Who, didn't like The Jam, then you didn't want to buy Ben Sherman, period. PAN PHILIPPOU

The role for the designers in this project was not just to change the space, but also, more significantly, to alter the identity of the brand and also radically challenge the perceptions of associations.

Brinkworth were invited to pitch for the job with seven other agencies. They won the project based on a presentation that recognised some of the fundamental aspects of the brand's appeal, but which recommended transforming and updating them to become something new for the twenty-first century. Ironically the first store to be transformed was the existing Ben Sherman store in the iconic Carnaby Street, London, home in the sixties to the mods with whom the brand had historically been most associated. It was in this location that the designers would test out the new spatial ideas.

In the early stages of the project, Brinkworth looked for British material associations with which to update the identity of the company. Iconic imagery centred upon the language of particular British spaces and their associated material forms: the pub, underground stations, social clubs, cafés, snooker halls and so on. All were social spaces that came with an associated and very particular aesthetic language. The glazed exterior tiles of pubs and their timber panelled interior, the ceramic motifs of the London Underground, tube stations, the pendant lights hanging over tables in the snooker hall and so on. All were selected highlights of very particular social spaces, all were places where the typical Ben Sherman customer may go, and all were places that were arguably enjoying a certain renaissance.

On this basis, Brinkworth settled on the very distinct image of the Brown Betty teapot. The crackled brown ceramic surface and its iconic form not only encapsulated what the new aesthetic could be, it also provided a riposte to the overwhelming dominance of the coffee shop, a space that was overtaking London at that time.

The complexities of reworking and updating a heritage brand ensured that careful analysis of the fundamental, and in some cases, successful aspects of the company needed to be retained and updated. In short, Ben Sherman wanted to retain its existing customers but also make new ones. One of the successful aspects of the brand was the iconic button-down Ben Sherman shirt. At the time of its redesign, 45% of Ben Sherman sales was in its shirts. Since its inception in 1963, the company had designed all of its own shirt fabrics; an archive of patterns that Brinkworth felt was a significant connection to its past, a fact that was important to communicate to its customers. As well as a core part of its service and a best seller, the shirt was the icon of the store. Therefore Brinkworth set out to place it centre-stage.

Like their work with AllSaints, Brinkworth decided that the new launch of Ben Sherman needed a powerful front of house statement. In order to elicit interest and curiosity, they reordered the entrance of the Carnaby Street store in order to shift the central door to the left-hand side to make room for a larger eye-catching window display.

In response, the window was filled with rows of shirts hung from a mechanical shirt-display rail, one that could be activated by buttons on the shop window and operated by passers-by. The visitor could choose numbered shirts that

would then be brought to the forefront of the display and rotated for viewing. This theatrical element of the storefront would regularly create crowds of shoppers eager to play with the machine. Once the interest of the passer-by was piqued, they then needed to be invited into the store and so make the connection between the street and the product. Therefore, the second aspect of the centrality of the garment to the project was the central positioning of the shirt bar.

Staffed by trained assistants, the shirt bar was a nod to the tailors of old, with 'know your collar sizes' and 'shirt of the week' inset into the wall of stacked garments. Like a bar to which young men would gravitate in a club or a pub, here, instead of being served with a drink, you could pick your favourite shirt: not just once, like a bespoke tailors, but time and time again. Shirt sales instantly went through the roof, growing by 40%, thus reinforcing the importance of the shirt to the brand and to the space.

SHIRT
OF THE WEEK

THE SH

PLECTRUM

BIRD

Spatial identities are often formed from numerous things. As well as the identity of the brand, the requirements of the client, the aesthetic predilections of the designer and the existing site can all play a major role in how the spaces are formed. Making spaces for the consumption of food add to the difficulties of creating distinct interiors. How can the particular taste and message of the food, the experience of its consumption, be externalised through space, materials and atmosphere?

BIRD is a fried chicken restaurant, which also serves waffles and is famous for its doughnuts and coffee served through a hatch to the street. It is dining that is quick and designed to impact on the taste buds of its diners through big flavours. Its interiors needed to match these gutsy approaches to the making and serving of food.

Collaborating with Michael Marriott on all three BIRD restaurants, each project started with the stripping back of the existing building in order to reveal the guts of the building. The intention was to match the strong and flavoursome food on offer with the surroundings in which it would be consumed. In the first BIRD on Kingsland Road, East London, the existing steel and bricks were exposed to be then juxtaposed with new checkerboard tiles and rough-timber banquet seats. Exposed air conditioning ductwork and pendant lighting cantilevered from the sidewall above the tables completed the raw aesthetic. Drawn from an inspirational image, green bottles were set into the walls underneath the windows, illuminating the interior with a green glow.

The selection of furniture was particularly important, and one that had to be judged just right. Furniture choices impact significantly on the design language and identity. Get it wrong and the choices send erroneous spatial signals, a mistake that can ruin an interior. The discussion about seating led to the use of the Windsor chair, which was a statement that encapsulated the projected identity of the company as well as the experience. On the corner of the restaurant a window was utilised to provide the first BIRD doughnut hatch, serving freshly baked cakes with coffee. Without having to either enter the restaurant or fully open it for business, food and drink can be served conveniently and directly out onto the street.

It's countryside meets urban. So, their key thing, BIRD, was their strap-line, it was, 'free-range and fried'. So, it was a slightly healthier, earthier, rural thing. It has got lipstick on it, and it's at the disco. MICHAEL MARRIOTT

I remember at the beginning, I proposed using a Thonet chair in high gloss lacquer. The client made this comment that I felt was spot on. He said, 'Isn't that more like French bistro?' I thought, 'Yes, you're right.' So that prompted a shift to the Windsor chair. One particular little bit was using a take on a '50s modernist version of a 19th-century Windsor chair. So, we'd had to slightly strip down a Windsor chair, which is like an ultimate country typology of seating. Then, getting it sprayed in high gloss, deep red. MICHAEL MARRIOTT

In the second BIRD in Islington a similar approach was taken in that the space was initially stripped back to its essential raw state and assessed for what this space offered. The building, a 1930s' pub located close to the Arsenal football ground, was designed with one eye on catering for large match-day crowds. The facade was restored in order to reveal the original glazed bricks, and white neon was used to sign the restaurant and announce it to its Holloway Road location. Inside, like Kingsland Road, a range of raw and rough materials applied in their natural state made the language of the brand and the unique qualities of the space combine. Against the rough exposed brickwork, a new main bar was constructed from perforated grey bricks, with a solid timber top. Behind the bar a steel frame holds bottles, glasses and various menu signage. One side of the restaurant houses private booths by the windows. Each blue table top is surrounded by a rolling wave of oak-timbered seating that culminates in a blackboard menu at the bar. A series of bright orange steel pendant lights illuminate each space and a perforated steel tray lights, holding fluorescent tubes, uplight the ceiling.

The centre of the restaurant was organised with the deployment of a series of high tables, inviting perching on the stools, or leaning on the top if in a hurry to eat before the match. The language of the perforated orange steel motif of the ceiling lights was carried on in the lights bolted to the table tops. The orange gloss aesthetic was even used on the small folded trays in which the condiments, menus and the serviettes needed when eating BIRD products are held.

A third BIRD in Camden carried on the juxtaposition of the distinct design language. In each of the BIRD spaces, the informality of the eating environment was combined with whatever the existing site offered after it had been excavated and exposed. It's a unique combination of both food and space that creates a distinct layering of taste, texture and brand.

FIORUCCI

Spaces to house iconic brands, replete with heritage and an illustrious history, can be challenging to design. How, if at all, should the history be exemplified? How much of the language or narrative of the heritage of the brand needs to be retained or utilised? Established in 1967 with three flagship stores in London, Milan and New York, Elio Fiorucci's famous fashion brand was bought in 2015 by Janie and Stephen Schaffer. They tasked Brinkworth with turning a 5500-square-foot ex-chocolate factory on the corner of Brewer and Great Windmill streets in Soho, London, into a new flagship store for the relaunch of the brand. Collaborating with the designers the Wilson Brothers, Brinkworth created a theatrical space that encapsulated the spirit of the brand's history, whilst representing it in an entirely new way.

When Adam called me following his initial meeting with Fiorucci, memories flooded back of our uncle (shoe designer Philip Wilson) returning from a trip to the Milano Fiorucci store in '84, complete with his photos of Keith Haring and LA2 painting. The conversation led to a jaw-dropping visual journey through the extensive Fiorucci graphics and cultural archive, resulting in a collaborative concept that celebrates the brand's heritage whilst keeping a firm eye on the future. OSCAR WILSON, WILSON BROTHERS

The two-level interior was organised as though a landscape of flamboyant events. Set against a neutral backdrop of timber flooring and white walls, the products, elements and objects of the brand were arranged to maximum effect. The space around the central circulation stair, embellished

with plants and a riot of neon lighting, housed a series of display elements enticing customers to the edges of the floors. A red circular bed, set on a circular tiled plinth with mirrored ceiling and vibrant curtain backdrop, was positioned to persuade customers to peruse an over-scaled shiny chrome rail of delicate, colourful underwear. The plinth carried on to accommodate a shoe display. Iconic Fiorucci clothing, such as T-shirts, was displayed in glass boxes, like museum pieces that could be picked up and tried on. Over-scaled display plinths were made to house jeans that were covered with trademark Fiorucci graphics.

Aware that Fiorucci is always moving forward and 'never finished' – a range of mobile mid-floor displays were conceived to sit alongside a remix-able ceiling-based visual system, allowing the space to adapt, adjust and evolve. BEN WILSON, WILSON BROTHERS

The whole interior of the shop was designed as a shiny, colourful fully reflective homage to the history of the brand but done in a way that transformed its identity for the 21st century;

Elio Fiorucci created his own visual universe for his shopper to dive into, a cheeky and cheerful utopia. Our concept for Brewer Street is an oasis of tropical optimism in a sea of dark times. If it was a record it would be 'Everybody loves the sunshine' by Roy Ayers. ADAM BRINKWORTH

VOODOO RAY'S

Named after the track by Manchester musician A Guy Called Gerald (who was invited to open the first Voodoo Ray's), the pizza-slice restaurant asked Brinkworth to further develop brand ideas into a series of spaces in various parts of London. Echoing some of the original ideas of the first Voodoo Ray's, on Kingsland High Street in Dalston, part of an ad-hoc assortment of shops and pubs, Brinkworth carried on the tradition of announcing the restaurant to the street with brash, bright neon signage. The red sign was a reminder of traditional pizza joints. The second restaurant picked up on this language and aesthetic metaphors for its new site situated in three containers in the Shoreditch Boxpark.

The long and thin container spaces determined the simple interior organisation. A counter ran across the three units fronting the kitchen space behind. Clad in blue tiles, the bar was easily seen as the customer entered the space. An entrance placed at either end of the three containers, meant that the units could accommodate long linear high tables on one side of each space. The middle unit, unencumbered by the movement of entering customers, could house two runs of tables: one on each side. Each were clad in different coloured glazed tiles. In order to increase the customer seating, some benches were placed in a small exterior yard externalising the restaurant interiors onto Shoreditch High Street.

The simplicity of the organisation belied the colourful identity of the interior. Utilising the signature tiling and colours established in the Dalston restaurant, Brinkworth reordered the perception of the linear spaces with bold geometric colour-tiled patterns. The candy-coloured, Memphis-like patterns suggested bold, cartoon-like impressions to the pizza eaters.

Pink and grey galvanised corrugated steel panels, placed diagonally in the first unit, were used to make a simple connection and a reminder between the interior and the shipping containers that they were placed within. Tall stools serviced the tiled surfaces of the long tables, each with a little pizza slice of colour removed, exposing their plywood substrate. In the third unit, a wall of pizza slices were reproduced in a simple graphic illustration cascading from the ceiling. The whole ensemble of riotous colour and shiny surfaces was lit with fluorescent lights emphasising the fast and playful atmosphere of the restaurant.

The third Voodoo Ray's in Camden carries on the interior ideas of bold colours and geometric shapes in order to create a fun and playful space in which to consume pizza by the slice!

I love architects and designers that work on a really low budget and figure out really creative solutions. In Voodoo Ray's, Brinkworth really went to town on tiling, and really getting geometric tiling to work in that space.
ROGER WADE, BOXPARK

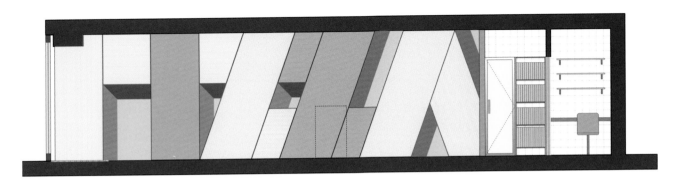

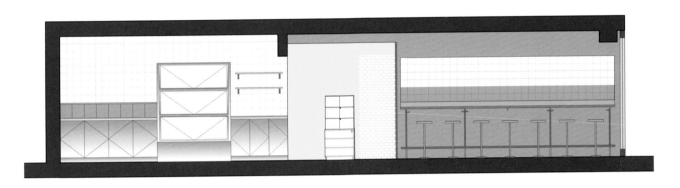

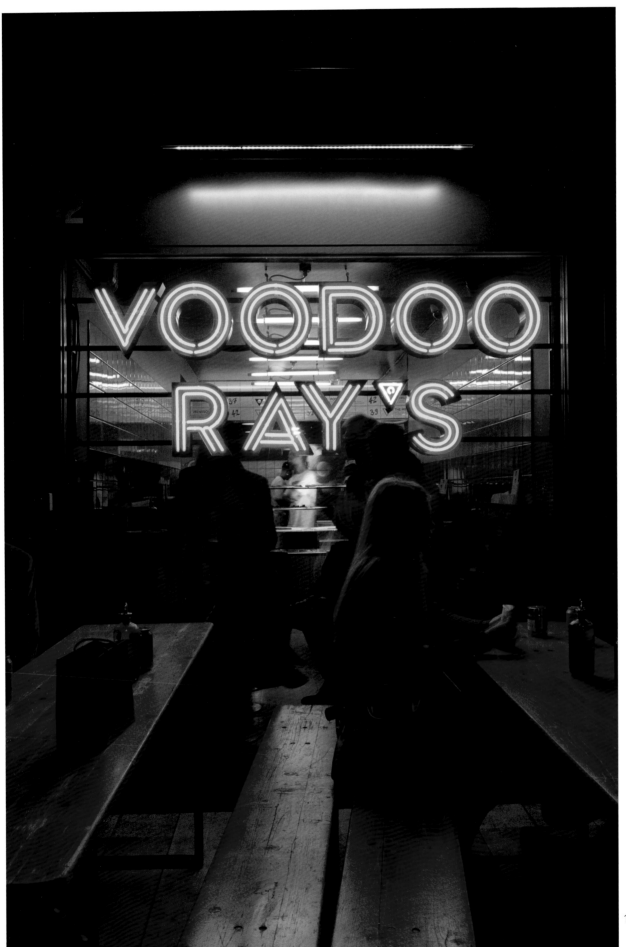

COMMUNITIES

The creation of unique spaces within which to accommodate a community of like-minded people, a group into similar experiences or things, or to house a place that personifies a particular company, or set of products, requires a thorough understanding of the community that you are designing for. It also requires an approach that is responsive to the challenges of these processes of transformation. To make spaces and environments that are explicitly tailored to a very particular group of people requires an ability for reflection and analysis: a sometimes challenging approach that will undertake a re-evaluation of your business, culture, community and so on.

Formed in 1962 by a group of designers and art directors, the D&AD foundation was set up to celebrate their work and also to raise the standards of their industry. Today, D&AD is a world-wide charity supporting numerous initiatives with well-established companies and designers as well as new talent. Its celebrated Yellow Pencil Awards are highly regarded accolades in the design industry. The foundation approached Brinkworth to design the new D&AD office in Cheshire Street, East London. The 8,000-square-foot two-level space was designed to house the D&AD staff, as well as to create an event space that could be used for in-house or external functions.

In this project the community of the workspace was exemplified through a robust approach to the existing building. A hole was punched through the concrete structure of the building in order to link the two floors, connecting the upper and lower levels. The material palette of the interior was understated. Cork, plywood, steel and peg-board echoed the aesthetics of the D&AD brand, mindful that, as a charity, an exuberant show of ostentatious materials would not sit comfortably with their philanthropic ethos. The project and the resultant space, exemplifies the foundation's working community, as well as providing a headquarters for its worldwide membership.

Brinkworth and Nike have worked together on numerous projects since 2002. Nike commissioned the practice, along with Phil Young of Prime and Fire, a sports, lifestyle and brand strategy consultancy, to work on the transformation of some tennis courts in Bermondsey. The courts were to be redesigned and a series of events were organised around Wimbledon 2016 in order to engage the local community to come and use the courts. Over the two-week event, Roger Federer and Serena Williams visited the new bright blue and pink courts, as well as the cargo crate club-house.

Whichever community is being spatialised, the organisation and selection of the relevant spaces, materials and elements with which to form the identities of the group, and the reflection of their culture back to them, is of paramount importance.

125

RAPHA

Simon Mottram, a keen cyclist who was an accountant and branding expert before he changed professions, founded Rapha in 2004. The product was launched with the Kings of Pain Exhibition in London: a month-long extravaganza focusing on six heroes of cycling who inspired the first clothing collection. Mottram's focus for the brand was on the production of better quality, stylish cycling gear, apparel that was not garish and poorly made. On his regular rides around Regent's Park, Mottram was acutely aware that low quality apparel was the only gear available to his fellow cyclists. During frequent post-ride coffees, he wondered if the obsessive attention to detail focused on their bikes could extend to clothes. From its inception Rapha was a hugely successful online retailer, and developed a very sophisticated identity with high quality products that were carefully marketed to a very discerning audience. This was achieved through the evolution of a community of fellow cycling enthusiasts and a knowledgeable company run by cyclists themselves who knew what the modern bike rider was interested in and also wanted.

Keen to evolve the online brand as a physical space, Rapha approached Brinkworth with a view to carefully creating an environment that emphasised the community and club ethic of the brand while enhancing the position and display of its quality cycling apparel. This was not done without some trepidation, as online-only brands often struggle with the switch to physical space: a less agile, more static environment and one associated with a different set of constraints and requirements in comparison to their presence in the digital world. Yet, because of the established nature of the brand, the exacting qualities of the client were of huge importance. It was up to Brinkworth to spatialise it.

The first Rapha clubhouse was in Brewer Street in Soho, London. It was strategically positioned to not only capture generous Soho footfall but also to be noticed and then utilised on the direct cycle route from Regent's Park to Bar Italia, just a few doors down. It was designed to perfectly encapsulate the relationship between high quality clothing and the best available coffee combining the two in a seamless space that emphasised two critically important aspects of modern cycling: the gear and the community of a cycling experience. In its first year the store was hugely successful, tripling estimated sales, and was extended to make more space for the social aspect of the club. Brinkworth had successfully synthesised the combination of social and sport in one space.

Central London retail environments are often designed in order to maximise every available space for display due to the demands of efficiency and costs. This approach often emphasises the mass-produced aspect of any interior. It is a method that can ensure that the customers regard the brand and the space exactly in that manner: cheap and numerous – a *hard-selling* space. Rapha and Brinkworth opted to reject this approach as it did not represent the company. Knowing that this was the antithesis of what this clubhouse should be, they carefully set about considering the customers' needs.

If you watch the barista making the coffee and getting the crema just right, it says something about the brand that's the same as the quality of stitching or the zip.

The last thing I wanted was a chain of, 'It's a Rapha cycle club clubhouse, it's the same. It's refreshingly familiar when I walk in.' I hate the idea of retail coming out of box and you just hang it up and then you trade.
SIMON MOTTRAM, RAPHA

What we really wanted was just professionalism, we wanted somebody who was really an expert in what they did so that they didn't make all the mistakes that we made ourselves. I expected them to grab the creative challenge, because it was a creative challenge. It's not, 'Do a shop for us.' It's, 'Create a clubhouse for us.' Which is a very different kind of project. I wanted somebody who would stretch us but be true to the brand.
SIMON MOTTRAM

RAPHA SEATTLE

COFFEE

ESPRESSO		3.00
MACCHIATO		3.50
AMERICANO		3.00
CAPPUCCINO		3.50
CORTADO		3.50
LATTE	3.50	4.00
MOCHA	3.75	4.25
DRIP	2.00	2.25
POUROVER		4.00
COLD BREW		4.25
CHAI	3.50	4.25
TEA (HOT) & ICED		4.25
HOT CHOCOLATE		3.50

LA CROIX	1.50
PELLEGRINO	3.50
ACQUA PANNA	3.50
COCA-COLA	3.00

FOOD

YOGURT & GRANOLA	3.50
ALMOND BUTTER TOAST	5.00
GOAT CHEESE & PROSCIUTTO TOAST	9.00
SALAMI SANDWICH	10.00
AVOCADO TOAST	8.00

This understanding manifested itself in a number of ways. As the cyclist enters the store, the front space is handed over to a cycle rack - allowing cyclists not to have to carry a heavy lock, fiddle with it outside and keep an eye on their bike. Some of the bikes entering this store cost the equivalent of a new car. Whilst a very simple gesture, this spatial generosity sets the scene for the clubhouse experience. In subsequent clubhouses, the bike rack has become the front signage of the shop, not only showing new visitors where the store is, but also, particularly in areas where external architectural alterations are restricted, it has become a welcoming invitation to the clubhouse.

This thoughtfulness continues throughout the clubhouse. Selected clothing and accessories are carefully laid out amongst historic bike parts, cycling magazines and information on rides and meets. The emphasis is on the information, education and the community of experts, both visiting and working in the space. Knowledgeable staff offer advice based on their own experience with the products. Much like Mottram, they test the stock on their rides, which in addition to giving them insight into the performance of the gear also enhances the club's atmosphere. They are armed with tablets to show stock and other ranges of products not out on display - ensuring that the digital aspect of the business is as much a part of the physical display, with both ensuring access to a more seamless connection between online information and physical space.

The community aspect of the clubhouse is also emphasised by the showing of races on a large screen in the space. Cycling events attract cyclists to the shop, who can enjoy a race, with good coffee and food, whilst perusing the clothing and accessories. To accommodate larger events and gatherings, display units in the space are flexible and can be moved freely on wheels. This allows the clubhouse to be adaptable, and to be changed during big cycling events such as the Giro d'Italia or the Tour de France.

The well-conceived clubhouse concept has now been reiterated in numerous other cities across the globe. The Rapha clubhouse ideas and pallet of materials are utilised as a guide for each of the stores that is adapted for an existing site and the cycling culture of each city. Whether Berlin, Seattle, Chicago or Tokyo, each store consists of a recognisable palette of Rapha ingredients: each remixed for the site and the city.

The exacting requirements of a knowledgeable client and the skills of Brinkworth have meant that each new clubhouse has furthered the spatial ambitions of the company.

Due to their successful partnership the clubhouse model is a huge success. However each one is realised, it is clear that they are environments that fuse a concept, the clothing and accessories, along with a club experience to a knowing community of particular expertise: an exemplary form of community engagement.

Simon was always clear that Rapha is about cycling. But 'cycling' in Mallorca is very different from 'cycling' in Seoul. One community has been doing it forever while for the other it's fairly new. Layer on that, the cultural differences between Spain and Korea, and you've instantly created two very different briefs for a clubhouse. Working with Rapha was an incredible opportunity to design for all these different cultures and communities, quite literally on opposite sides of the world, but that all have this one thing in common. To go and put the same design into every space across the world wouldn't have made any sense.
LISA CRUTCHLEY, ASSOCIATE DIRECTOR

Sometimes we will be our own worst enemy because we'll go 'Well that's not Rapha.' Brinkworth are very good, I think, at challenging that. 'Well don't you think we could push it here? How about this?' They get it right. That's been the best thing they've done, to push that line really well.
SIMON MOTTRAM

BOXPARK

After creating numerous pop-up retail spaces in various trade fairs in his previous role as the originator of Box Fresh, Roger Wade wondered if he could avoid having to undertake the same process time and time again. He was also concerned about avoiding the excess waste produced by each show break-down. Wade formulated ideas regarding creating a temporary space, one that could be shipped in a container to each show that was ready-packed and easy to assemble. This evolved into extending this idea to a ready-packed shopping and eating experience, a place that could be deployed quickly and expediently, yet create maximum impact upon its users. The first Boxpark was designed and built alongside a slither of land beside Shoreditch High Street station in 2011. Described as the first 'pop-up shopping mall', it was originally conceived to last just five years: it is still operating today. It fulfilled Wade's idea of transience and temporality, as well as the expedience of making ready-made spaces.

Boxpark utilised an off-the-peg, ready-made element: the shipping container. The shipping container is a ubiquitous object, cheap and plentiful, yet easily adapted for reuse and able to be fitted out for a whole variety of uses. Consisting of 60 shipping containers, spread over two floors, the Shoreditch Boxpark contained 48 shops, bars and restaurants. The exterior of the containers was finished in matt black with bold graphics applied to the side. Brinkworth reworked the upper level of the Shoreditch Boxpark in 2017, to 'winterise' it, and make it habitable all year round.

The Shoreditch prototype was so successful that a second Boxpark was opened in Croydon in 2016. Utilising a similar approach to Shoreditch, reworking meanwhile or leftover space, adjacent to infrastructure such as a train station, awaiting redevelopment in the near future, this time the Croydon Boxpark forms part of a BDP/Brinkworth designed larger urban masterplan alongside the station. Less pop-up and more integrated into the development, it has been formed out of 96 containers and the boxes are arranged around a central covered courtyard. It is a huge space filled with tables and benches, much like a European street market. The communities of Croydon are brought together to enjoy various street foods, entertainment and shops under one large glazed roof.

The success of the model means that a third Boxpark will open in late 2018 and will not only house the usual restaurants, bars and retail spaces, it will also contain a 2000-person event space. Based in Wembley Park it will also contain 26 studio spaces, for up and coming designers and artists: a response to the lack of affordable studio space available in London.

The Boxpark model creates community through the utilisation of the shipping container – a ubiquitous, everyday, to-hand object. It is a radically simple yet obvious response to the creation of places where people can come together and participate in life. Brinkworth's role in evolving this community-based space was to rethink and repurpose the shipping container. It was an exercise in taking a ready-made found object and utilising its qualities to extract the maximum effect from an off-the-shelf object. It is an expedient approach, and one that personifies great interior design, a discipline that is based upon the reworking of the contingencies of existing sites and materials.

I think with Boxpark, we're, first and foremost, a design and a consumer-led company. Our thing is about creating special experiences. That's very much at the heart of it. ROGER WADE, BOXPARK

Why expend energy and build something from scratch when perfectly acceptable and off-the-shelf objects and solutions are already to hand?'
CRAIG MARTIN, SHIPPING CONTAINER (OBJECT LESSONS)

DIESEL VILLAGE

A ready-made approach to the design of interior space can be useful for a number of reasons. Firstly, it can be economically prudent: existing materials and objects can be sourced from any supplies. Secondly, it can be extremely expedient: ready-made solutions speed up costly design and construction time. The usual processes of thinking and making, where origination and fabrication dominate, instead involve a different set of approaches: methods where the selection, edit and construction of the objects and elements will make discerning design statements.

Brinkworth were approached to design a large pop-up temporary Diesel flagship store on Regent's Street, London. A Grade II listed status on the existing site meant that the 5,000-square-foot two-floor space had to be completed without significantly altering the existing structure. To complicate matters further, it had to be designed and made quickly and in time for the Christmas sales period. On a very limited budget, working with the Wilson Brothers, the project began with a meticulous documenting of the Diesel range, separating it out into related product groups. Each grouping of products was then assigned a space. The resultant process suggested that each space was assigned its own form: in other words, an approach that created a *village* of environments.

A powerful design strategy is the use of the ready-made, an approach that utilises the existing as a signifier or metaphor for the new space being constructed. In other words, when a ready-made approach is utilised, the selection and edit of the off-the-peg object can be made with a particular aesthetic and functional choice in mind. This approach can also maximise the contrast and tension between the existing context and any new activity in it. Ready-mades are chosen not just for expediency but also for the message that they convey. Usually ready-mades are utilised because they are objects or elements that have been removed from their original context, thus a powerful resonance can be formed essentially through the fact that the environment is made with elements that were never usually intended to be located in that environment. This was the approach for the Diesel Village project.

For each environment in which to house the discreet ranges an off-the-peg solution was found in the use of a basic everyday garden greenhouse. Each of the greenhouse structures were adapted in order to complement the qualities of the products that they were housing. Metallic iridium glazing was used in the reflective and colourful watches area, rough-sawn timber for hats and T-shirts, clear glazing with fluorescent tube-lights for shirts and jeans, and so on. The village environments were sometimes manipulated in order to make new openings, or cladding panels were left on in order to make new ways of entering and moving through the spaces. Greenhouses were also utilised for the cash and wrap area, and the changing rooms. The structures were placed selectively within the two levels of the interior, and in such a way as to emphasise the contrast between the existing building and the new elements.

In order to extract the maximum theatricality of this approach, and to ensure that the village of shelters was clearly understood as separate to the structure of the building, the existing shell of the ground floor menswear level was sprayed dark grey. The upper level womenswear floor was finished in a lighter grey. The existing staircase was clad in Valchromat: black medium density fibreboard (MDF). Strip lighting and bold adhesive vinyl graphics were also applied to the structures to ensure not just a coherently branded environment but also to create a memorable interior statement.

As well as the spatial impact, the bold and cost-effective project was designed to create a high-impact social media statement, one that ultimately ensured Diesel could demonstrate that their products were to be consumed in a very particular manner and environment. The dynamic imagery of the store achieved this: it was not only an impressive spatial statement, but also a social media hit. The success of this project in its delivery, installation and ultimately reception meant that its life was extended by an additional month. This ensured that the 'village community' could be enjoyed for a longer period during the visual overload of the Christmas celebrations.

SUPREME

James Jebbia founded skateboarding brand Supreme in 1994, with its first store opening on Lafayette in New York City. The approach to the early store design was simple yet pragmatic. The concept was to focus on the product and to give it space to breathe. Therefore all of the clothes and accessories were placed around the perimeter of the store. This simple idea has become a trademark approach for the design of the subsequent stores: the conception of a free space, where the product is important but also where the community it appeals to is welcomed easily into the space.

Brinkworth were commissioned to design the London store in 2011 and subsequently the Paris store in 2016. Both were collaborations with the Wilson Brothers. Akin to Supreme's brand, both spaces were enigmatic and certain features cut across the accepted norms of retail design and the display of products. In Paris, the existing site presented a unique problem in that it was a small room at the front of the building connected to a larger backroom via a corridor. Whilst the backroom was generous and top-lit with a large steel and glass structure, the unorthodox set of spaces meant that unusual solutions needed to be generated in order to combine the two distinct rooms.

Supreme has a long history of collaborating with artists and designers with whom they can develop and decipher their products. In particular they have commissioned artists such as Damian Hirst, Jeff Koons and the Chapman brothers to make one-offs for the company. This exceptional history of objects was utilised to create a carefully curated linear display of boards: a set of objects placed on the wall that ran from the front to the back of the space, and which linked the two spaces together. In one move the distinctive separate rooms were connected with a timeline of curated objects. The front room needed to act as a distinctive attraction for the passer-by. A tall sculpture by skateboarder Mark Gonzales of a priest provided just this, as did wall art by 'Weirdo Dave', consisting of numerous images plastered onto the wall. As the visitor traverses the rooms via the corridor, they move towards the tall, illuminated backroom and to the simple yet finely engineered display of products, above which an artwork by Gonzales was painted directly on the wall.

BAYSIXTY6

I really like BaySixty6, just because I like the fact that they did that. It has a lot of Adam in it. You know he's a skater, you know he loves that and for him that would be a dream project. They delivered it in such a way that, I can't really think anyone else could or should have done it better.
ADRIAN CADDY, GREENSPACE

The legendary BaySixty6 skate park has occupied a unique location under the Westway flyover in London since the late 1990s. But whilst skating and the design of parks had become more complex and sophisticated in their demands, BaySixty6 had not. In order to ensure that this classic park continued to inspire future riders, it needed to change.

Appointed by brand/event agency Urb-Orbis on behalf of Nike, Brinkworth, along with Phil Young, were presented with a unique opportunity to help resurrect the park, updating it for a new generation of skaters. Challenged to develop a scheme that encouraged a spirit of inclusion and community, they reworked the complete layout of the site to offer the best possible skateable area, whilst improving the amenities offered to enhance the experience for both skaters and non-skaters alike.

Consolidating the new ramps and obstacles to a single area of the park ensured that the expanse of the site could be celebrated, championing the park's core activity - skating. Importantly, lines of sight were designed to be uninterrupted across the entire park, save for the impressive structure of the Westway motorway sitting above the park. This maximised the visibility for spectators during competitions and demos and at the same time improved safety for the participants.

Brinkworth worked closely with one of the world's best timber skate park designers and builders, Skatepark Amsterdam (NDSM), who were tasked by Urb-Orbis to design, develop and build a set of ramps and obstacles that would ensure the place of BaySixty6 as one of the leading skate parks in the UK. To achieve this, a number of unique features were specifically produced for BaySixty6,

catering for a broad range of skaters across all levels of skill and ability. A hydraulic box was installed, which allowed the height to be adjusted at the push of a button - meaning it can be set to suit any level. Another feature is a new kicker ramp, directly in front of a viewing window, offering spectators the chance to catch a glimpse of boarders as they fly past. Another was an impressive bowl, featuring innovative hexagonal corner panels, offering the smoothest and most fluid ride possible.

To complement the vast improvements in the skateable areas, Brinkworth developed the facilities to include a shop and a canteen that doubles up as an educational space, housed within brightly painted green shipping containers. These are positioned so as to back onto the ramps with a window framing sightlines down the spine of the skate park making it an ideal shelter for spectators in any weather conditions.

These new facilities were strategically positioned around a central courtyard - a communal zone clad in recycled decking and containing bench seating, where visitors can congregate to socialise or unite as part of organised events. The clean and utilitarian space was intended to be used as a flexible venue, a blank canvas to host events such as premier skate films or exhibitions. The shop, developed by Brinkworth specifically for BaySixty6, mixed concrete wall panels and walnut shelves to offer a sophisticated pallet not regularly associated with skate shops; further reflecting Nike's commitment to elevating the overall perception of the park.

One of the most iconic parts of Brinkworth's scheme is a graphic approach to lighting throughout the site. The creative yet functional application of fluorescent tubes follows the contours of the Westway's dramatic concrete underbelly overhead. BaySixty6 was transformed into an inclusive and stimulating skate park, animated by the numerous riders who use it daily, ensuring its legacy will continue to inspire generations and attract more and more skaters to the ramps and to the community of users.

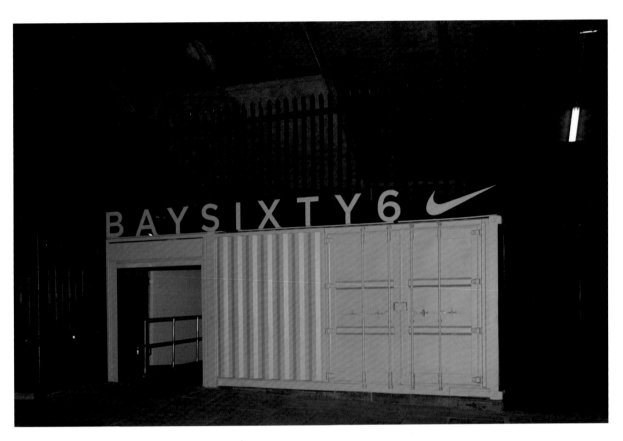

BROWNS EAST

After a call to the studio, Ad, Ray and I met Holli to hear her visionary brief for the retail store of the future. Excited but with no time, only three days, we took the radical approach to return to pitch with a sketchbook full of ideas. They were impressed with our quick turnaround of designs, which married with their vision. We were on board, but it was a sprint to deliver a challenging and an ever-changing brief; a pop up, not a pop up, a gallery, event space, café, gender-neutral, completely flexible, community and a VIP shopping area. The space we delivered is art itself. We took great care in the design and engineering of beautifully bespoke sculptural pieces that seamlessly transform the space, fit for purpose and worthy of adorning suitably designer price tags. It's a pleasure to have worked on and visit regularly, if only to window shop.
KAREN BYFORD, MANAGING DIRECTOR

In the 21st century, notions of community can be extended to describe the intangible online presence of people and of places. Like many others, Brinkworth's work in the exploration of the relationship between digital and physical spaces involves the complex investigation into how both impact upon space in the design of retail environments. Browns East was designed to be an exemplar of the integration between e-commerce and physical space.

Browns is a London fashion icon, around since the 1970s when it opened its South Molton Street store. Browns East, a new venture, occupies 4,000 square feet of two floors in a former print factory in Shoreditch. Their first new store for over 20 years, the shop is an augmented space in that it works seamlessly with the digital online presence of the brand. A Browns app allows customers to share their history with the store and can tailor their preferences, as well as ensuring stock is made available almost immediately if not in store when the customer visits. (Radio stock tracking means that anything that is not in store can be ordered and delivered within 60 minutes.)

In opening Browns East, we are building on our strong pioneering heritage, with innovation at the heart of our approach. We appointed Brinkworth to lead the design for Browns East as we have always respected their incredible talent for architecture and brand design. We felt that partnering on this new venture was the perfect opportunity to establish a new blueprint for the future of retail.
HOLLI ROGERS, CEO OF BROWNS

The store itself, a gender-neutral environment, was designed to be flexible and which could be reordered quickly and efficiently in order to incorporate new ranges or to show displays from a fresh new design talent. A series of sculptural product display elements, inspired by the 1930s Polish Avant Garde artist Katarzyna Kobro, follows a rigor of geometric principles, which in turn enables them to be reconfigured for brand take-overs and product storytelling. Each were made to be utilised individually or combined to make numerous configurations. Their endless potential for reconfiguration allows the store to be able to be constantly transformed in order to tell a new story about the products that are being displayed.

It is great to work with a client who has such strong and forward-thinking ideas, who gives you the space and trust to create something unique together. I had never worked with such a varied material palette, but we had great fun finding the right tones, textures; playing with reflections and contrast. ANA VARELA, ASSOCIATE DIRECTOR

It is very flattering to have been asked to design a new landmark for this iconic retailer and it's been a real pleasure working with their talented and inspiring team. We re-addressed the use of this charming building and introduced a set of tools in the form of freestanding elements that facilitate varying retail moments. This approach enables Browns East to be an exciting and ever-changing host to their Shoreditch customer. ADAM BRINKWORTH

CONVERSE

Brands will often sponsor events in order to develop a closer connection between product and consumer. By doing this they hope to facilitate deeper associations between product and user. Converse identified two music festivals in London that they wanted to be a part of in order to reach and connect to their target audience. Both were aimed at a specific group of 15 to 30 year olds, a target audience for the trainer brand who wanted to re-ignite their credentials as an edgy, credible company that made footwear that was appealing to youthful sub-cultures.

Converse approached Brinkworth and tasked them with creating a place that would embrace the community of users and allow them to fully engage with Converse. They decided to do this through creating a temporary enclosure that housed a customising station: a place where the festival goers could customise their Converse trainers through printing, weaving, riveting, painting and stamping. This idea began with the iconic Chuck Taylor boot and the star, originally an ankle protector, on the outside of the shoe. Brinkworth turned this feature of the shoe inside out so the star was now on the inside of the shoe and the wearer was encouraged to customise their shoes creatively and individually.

Brinkworth were interested in the relatively lo-tech footwear of the company. Considering this difference of engineering and aesthetic, the designers decided that the simple, non-precious approach to remaking and customising shoes would be housed in a simple no-nonsense off-the-peg structure, one that would stand out in the festival environs yet at the same time ensure that it spoke the same language as the community that it was trying to attract. In addition, the structure was to be staffed by people who could already have been at the festival and DJs, graffiti artists and illustrators would be on-hand to help the community customise their shoes.

As is often the case in a temporary structure approach, expediency and cost-effectiveness were of paramount concern. The structure also had to adapt to the two festival sites and therefore be able to change its layout for each one: L-shaped in one, rectangular in the other. The structure also needed to appear to be relatively simple and lo-tech, yet at the same time relatively sophisticated in order to complement the hi-tech technology that was to be housed inside the structure. With all these factors considered, the pop-up was constructed out of simple, ready-made materials.

The basic structure was formed from a galvanised key-clamp black metal frame. Where protection was needed from the weather, twin-wall polycarbonate sheeting was used as roofing. Oriented Strand Board (OSB) panels were used both in raw and black-stained form in order to make both the cladding for the structure as well as a series of small, low, bench seating and table furniture. Recycled compressed wood-chip palettes, moulded with a highly modulated and distinctive surface, were painted black and utilised as a cladding for the frame to make a space for the printers and customising equipment. The off-the-peg quality of the palettes, usually found in warehouses being shifted around the factory floor by forklift trucks and laden with stacks of products, appealed to Brinkworth as they were reminiscent of the off-the-peg qualities of the Chuck Taylor shoe – Converse's classic and the first shoe they produced. The interior of the room housed the technology and also the displays of shoes – some of which were hung from the ceiling.

As well as acting as a formal device for the layout of the enclosure, the tower in the structure had a functional purpose in that it was created in order to house the stock of shoes, as well as to host a DJ booth. On the side of the tower was a basketball hoop – another draw for the festival goers.

Through the simple steel, wood and palette structure, Brinkworth created a temporary space that attracted the community of festival goers to their site. The building exemplified the product and synthesised the opportunity for its users to not only customise their shoes but to participate in the co-creation of their festival experience.

FUTURES

STUDIO FUTURES

FROM BETHNAL GREEN:

What I am interested in is how to have better space. How I think it is going to change us is that I think it is going to develop not just as a space for us to work, I think it is going to be a better space for our clients to come and work with us. So there are two floors on the top, and I am going to encourage the clients to stay, have a meeting, meet in our office, improve the hospitality, make the studio an activation design space that works on building relationships.
ADAM BRINKWORTH

We like that Wilson Brothers is WB, and Brinkworth is BW. They are like the fourth Wilson Brother to us.
OSCAR WILSON, WILSON BROTHERS

Brinkworth are embarking on a new future. Not only are they planning an extension to the Bethnal Green studio, designed by Michael Gollings, they now have an office in New York. As well as the physical additions, their work always needs to be anticipating what is next in the fields of design they are engaged in. In order to stay ahead, attributes such as design agility, responsiveness and a keen sensibility for what is new are critical attributes needed to survive. So, what does the future look like for Brinkworth? Where will it take them?

Currently in planning, the studio is being adapted to become a host of not just the practice but clients, collaborators, co-workers. A place where people can come and spend more time with the practice, extending the unique Brinkworth welcome. Whilst in another continent, the characteristics of the New York office are not a million miles away from Bethnal Green.

TO BROOKLYN:

My son's friend's dad runs a furniture company called Uhuru Design, and they have a space in Brooklyn where they design and make furniture. They said they have some space on Red Hook pier, an amazing old warehouse. I went

over to take a look and right next door was a motorcycle repair shop, with 200 bikes outside ranging from Harleys to Triumphs, I thought ... this is it. Before I even saw the space. DEREK O'CONNOR, CEO BRINKWORTH INC.

The office in Red Hook, Brooklyn, is being run by Derek O'Connor. Undaunted by his task, he is determined to imprint the Brinkworth characteristics into the new context and infuse it with a North American flavour.

Brinkworth bring amazing creativity, humbleness to their approach, very down to earth people and spaces, a real rigor for quality, they talk about materials in a way that nobody else does. They want to make spaces that work and have longevity. This is the challenge, how do we integrate the behaviours that are coming, new technologies where mobile devices are playing an increasing role in how they shop, in their daily lives how do Omni-channel behaviours translate into Brinkworth spaces?
DEREK O'CONNOR

WORK FUTURES

The things we're doing at the moment are all influenced by new technology and how it changes the way we relate to everything around us, which fascinates me. This evolution, especially in retail design, is evident in people's behaviour and therefore affects how we design spaces to embrace that. Having worked with Google and then with Facebook, I can see the potential of future change. It's about splicing together digital and physical spaces that deliver environments to build brand communities.
ADAM BRINKWORTH

Digital technologies, especially in retail, have impacted significantly on the design of interior space. Keeping ahead of this change is critical. Brinkworth can see it and are already exploring what it means. Clients and collaborators are already aware of its pressing demands and are reacting accordingly. Brinkworth are already heavily involved in innovating in this field.

It's really interesting. I think the next thing that's going to be really challenging is digital and physical and how we sensitively bring along, and channel, experience to the physical space. Last year, Brinkworth did the most brilliant presentation about the future of the clubhouse that just showed that they were so far ahead of anybody else we talked to. SIMON MOTTRAM, RAPHA

All aspects of branded space are being impacted upon by changes in behaviour. Responses are beginning to emerge in the way Brinkworth are designing seamless spaces, where boundaries between the digital and the existing are rendered as delimited. It's almost as if the endless interior, where the limits as to where the physical interior begins and ends, is now here:

The physical spaces that brands create are about building that customer relationship. They are telling you narrative stories, they're vying for your attention, inviting you to events, showing you their next product, what's online. So social media, the physical spaces and the product, should all be combined, they are all vehicles for them all to be seen in an instant. KEVIN STANFORD, ALLSAINTS, KAREN MILLEN

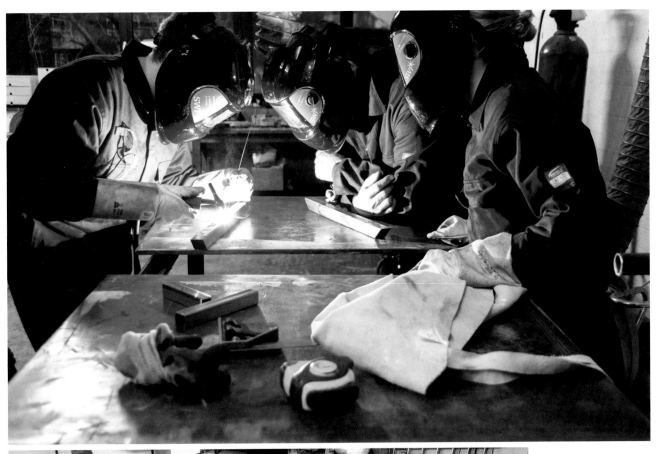

PEOPLE FUTURES

We've all grown now and have other lives as well but it's still family. I've spent more time with these guys than anyone else in my life. HOWARD SMITH, PRACTICE DIRECTOR

I knew it was going to be a very different experience from the other studios I had worked for. It was like a new beginning / new chapter for me and I got stuck in. Lots of travelling, lots of responsibility, lots of balancing communication, lots of thinking, rationalising, lots of learning, lots of rewarding and fulfilling fun times. For me Brinkworth represented creativity, they became my world and family all at once. RACHEL BOWYER, NEW BUSINESS DIRECTOR

I can't believe it's 20 years but they have been the best! We have all grown together over the years and I can't imagine life without Brinkworth in it! I really can't thank Adam and Kevin enough for making me feel part of their family! We are not only working colleagues we are great friends too ... We know we will always be there for each other! DIANE HORAN-HILL, FINANCE DIRECTOR

I would say that for the oldies, Adam, Kevin, Diane, Louise and myself there is a feeling of all having grown up together. PAT MEAGHER, CONSULTANT

When I started at Brinkworth 20 years ago, it was a very different place. There were 9 of us back then, 1 computer, 1 fax machine, and the toilet was outside in the backyard which was full of pigeons. Half the space was an office the other half a workshop full of machinery. Kevin and Diane joined shortly after. It has been amazing to see the company grow and evolve, see people come and go, seeing briefs land and awesome projects designed and realised. It's pretty legendary what Brinkworth has achieved. I can't help but feel gushing and nostalgic when I think back over the years as well as proud and honoured to be part of this journey. LOUISE MELCHIOR, PR DIRECTOR, PHOTOGRAPHER

The beginning of the Brinkworth journey incorporated the connections between thinking and making. In a circuitous narrative, Brinkworth have developed a workshop where staff have welding lessons, make stuff, understand materials. It's called *Brinkworks.*

I think there's a resurgence of interest in making from a number of levels. Architects, designers, wanting to do more hands-on stuff. It's people like Assemble, young groups. Or even architects/artists/theatre set designers, getting together and doing projects. Then also I think there are people like Brinkworth, intentionally looking at a way to incorporate a workshop as part of their thing. I think within product furniture design, there are more people who are coming at it as designers, not as craftspeople. They're using craft, and making technologies to achieve their works. Some of that is partly to do with that world of galleries selling design ... Essentially, people just get absolutely bored and fed up with being at a screen all day in practice. MICHAEL MARRIOTT

In response to the resurgence in making, and as a reaction to the reliance on the digital, Brinkworks is a facility where staff can develop their thinking in the relationship between space, material, the digital and the real. Making is coming to the fore again.

It's more about the hands on approach, rather than focusing on beautiful visuals. We are noticing more and more that candidates coming out of universities are very narrowly focussed on 3D visualisation which is a problem for us. By getting into the workshop we hope to look more at the tactile, how people use and interact with our work. SONNY CANT, DIRECTOR

For a company that is very people-orientated, how they evolve their future workforce, collaborators and clients is extremely important. How they see themselves in the wider community is also critical.

I think the fact that it's here in Bethnal Green and knowing the neighbourhood, and just being part of this area is a big thing for all of us. LUCY PORTER, PR MANAGER

And, finally, what about the futures of the people who originated the company:

Success? Be happy, and be the best version of myself would be a good one wouldn't it? I never stop to think am I successful or not. And inherently, because of my insecurities I don't feel successful. I fear it is all going to go to shit, so I keep on going ... ADAM BRINKWORTH

I've got a place in Reykjavik I'm building. I'd love to just go and spend a month doing a project, then come back and build it, you know what I mean? That is such a romantic idea. We've got an office in New York now. Go to New York, spend a month there, a month in London, a month in Iceland and then holiday in between, that'd be ideal. KEVIN BRENNAN

Postscript.
He doesn't like to wear buttons.
OSCAR WILSON, WILSON BROTHERS

DESIGNING INTERIORS SERIES

This curated series will set out new emergent thinking in the fields of interior design and architecture in the form of monographs on contemporary designers' work. The designers and practices included in the series are award-winning and widely perceived to be leading firms of international reputation. The series will establish a canon of exemplary interior architects, designers and decorators who have made distinguished contributions to the realisation of inside spaces.

ACKNOWLEDGEMENTS

In 2016 I asked Adam if he wanted his company to be the first in a series of interior monographs that I wanted to publish on great design practices, and that I would like to talk to him about possible authors for the project. I was taken aback (and also secretly delighted) by his response: 'if we were to do this, then we would want you to write it'. When interviewing Adam and Kevin, their clients, colleagues, staff, friends, I realised that this was part of the way they worked: they chose people they wanted to work with and were direct about it, seeking out collaborators whose work they enjoyed, or, at least, thought interesting. I was flattered, and still am. It has been an honour and a pleasure to work with Brinkworth, and to spend time in their world. It's a special privilege to feel like a collaborator in this amazing story. Thank you doesn't cover it, but lots of them all the same. As well as the Brinkworth team, special thanks to Lucy for helping, arranging and generally being there when needed, and, of course, thank you to all of the practice - staff, colleagues, clients, collaborators - all wonderful people who gave up so much of their time for interviews. Many thanks to Stephanie Rebello, Val Rose and Sarah Thorowgood at Lund Humphries, for supporting this project, and to FUEL for the great design. As always, thank you to Claire and Mr Osgood.

GRAEME BROOKER

BRINKWORTH STAFF PAST AND PRESENT

Adam Brinkworth, Adrian Thompson, Afraz Naqvi, Aimee Taylor, Alasdair McNab, Alex Clifford, Alex Etchells, Alex Holden, Alexander Gardner, Alexandra Cragg, Alexandra Edwards, Ali McCulloch, Alice Adamczewski, Amanpreet Shokar, Amy Tipper, Ana Varela Fernandez, Andrea Tohill, Andrew Shove, Andrew Stafford, Andy Knowles, Ani Chepakova, Anita Peto, Anja Haerter, Anna Perrity, Antoine Phelouzat, Antonio Barcelos, Armelle Goury, Arnar Sigurjonsson, Ashley Craik-Collins, Ashley McFarlane, Ashley Scarborough, Ashley Waring, Ben Assefa-Folivi, Ben Ayres, Ben Paul, Bodrul Khalique, Brooke Carden, Camilla Wood, Candy Stanton, Carl Clerkin, Carl Nicholls, Carla Brown, Caroline Broadbridge, Caroline Campbell, Caroline Collett, Catherine Warmann, Catrin Morgan, Chris Hall, Chris Simmons, Christopher Hall, Claire Miller, Coretta Van Wijk, Curro Perez Alcantara, Dan Rees, Dan Savage, Dan Wilson, Daniel Camacho, Danielle Van Rhijn, Danny Osbourne, Daryl Sheridan, David Bennett, David Hurren, Declan McGabbhan, Delroy Herron, Derek O'Connor, Diane Hill, Dylan Luke, Ebba Fox, Elaine McQuaid, Eldina Begic, Elif Duztepe, Eliza Downes, Elliot Morris, Emilie Chen, Emily Howarth, Emma Merrit, Emma Payne, Emma Sproul, Emma Whitcomb, Emma Wynn, Ethelinde Radloff, Eva Siekmann, Felicity Lam, Felicity Toop, Finlay Bourke, Gabriella Gillard, Gary Gahan, Gary Nash, Geoff Stewart, George Knott, George Woolaghan, Gof Sasit, Grace Patton, Graham Russell, Hannah Cackett, Harvin Alert, Heather Potter, Helena Stolpe, Henry Flitton, Henry Hagger, Howard Smith, Ian Sumner, Ian Thompson, Isabella Lang, Jack Sharp, Jake Powley-Baker, James Taylor, James Harris, James Mason, James Scott, James Thormod, Jane Miller, Jeanette Allen, Jennifer Campbell, Jenny Andersson, Jenny McFarthing, Jess Gray, Jo Adams, Jo Ash , Jo Brinkworth, Jo Gomm, Jo Hinds, John Stead, Johnny Mangham, Jonathan Goss, Jono Woolf, Jordan Mirchov, Jude Hart, Jude Whyte, Julianna Loboda, Julien Antonescu Ladaret, Julien Delannoy, Julius Brinkworth, Karen Byford, Karl Piper, Kat Ekstrom, Kate Brewer, Kate French, Katherine Malouf, Katie Askew, Katie Pengilly, Kevin Brennan, Kevin Hubbard, Kieran Morgan, Kirk Le Voi, Kostas Xenos, Laetita Vaile, Lara Sparey, Laura Ashford, Laura Cant, Laura Ceriani, Laura Greig, Laura King, Lauren Slevin, Leila Ringrose, Libby Allen, Linda Raimondo, Lindsey Bell, Lisa Crutchley, Lisl Du Toit, Liv Engelhardt, Lloyd Spencer, Louise Melchior, Luca Mantovanelli, Lucy Jackson, Lucy Porter, Luke Chapman, Luke Ward, Marc Duffy, Maria Marinho, Marnie Brinkworth, Matt Davies, Matt Humphrey, Matt Naylor, Max McDougall, Meg O'Hara, Melanie Massey, Melanie Richardson, Melanie Riepl, Melvin Gibbons, Michael Whitton, Miho Sakamoto, Milly Wood, Min-sung Kim, Murray Aitken, Nabila Halimuwdin, Nadia Micallef, Nalini Di Taverni, Natalie Bell, Natalie Clay , Natalie Ow, Nataliya Shkarupa, Natasha Greenleigh, Natasha Marley, Nick Delo, Nick Pope, Nick Roberts, Nicola Fenech, Ola Pasowicz, Oliver Hawkes, Owen Nichols, Paddy Austin, Pamela Flanagan, Pat Meagher, Patiya Pullket, Peter Griffith, Philip Gay, Philip Stewart, Polina Abery, Rachel Bowyer, Rhona Waugh, Richard Blurton, Rob McCombie, Roisin Reilly, Rowena Mbanu, Ruby Asare-Brown, Ryan Leedham, Ryan Thomas, Sacha Kemp-Potter, Sait Saitoglu, Sam Derrick, Sam Hosker, Sam McMorran, Sam O'Donohue, Sam Tipper, Samantha Dufee, Sandra Canabate, Sara Brockett, Sara Stanton, Sarah Clayton, Sarah Shipley, Scott Compton, Shakera R., Shammimma Ahmed, Sigrid Andest, Sigrun Sverrisdottir, Silka Gebhardt, Simon Ash, Sonny Cant, Steph Mount, Steve Dingui, Steve Wynn, Supisara Pupunwinwat, Tanja Hitzemann, Tish Vail, Toby Sendall, Tom Drew, Tom Russell, Tommy Miller, Tracey Graham, Tracey Halliday, Treena Boon, Vicky Morse, Vince Kwan Tsang, Will Hardie, Will Kent, Will Whiteaway, Xander Gardner.

This book is dedicated to the memory of our dear friends
Carl Nicholls and Bodrul Khalique.

All photography © Louise Melchior

Except:
p15, visuals on p164–165: Gollings Architects
p17 (top), p19–21: Jose King
p18, p31 (top right), p57 (top right and bottom), p70 (top),
p131 (bottom right): Brinkworth
p37: stills from film by Arlen Figgis
p38, p40–41: Oscar Wilson
p44 (top left): JB Guesne
p44 (top right, middle): Carl Clerkin
p44 (bottom): Fiona Banner
p45 (top): Jack Hems
p45 (bottom right): Hugo Glendinning
p45 (bottom left): photo by Magis Photo: Tom Vack
p49 (bottom): Fresh Britain
p51, p69, p70 (bottom), p71-73, p127 (top): Alex Franklin
p55: Paul Tyagi
p61 (top and bottom): Modern House
p67 (top): Alex James
p75: Sirli Raitma
p84–85: Peter Cook
p101 (top), p151, p154 (top): Ed Reeve
p125 (bottom), p127 (bottom): Jonathan Savoie
p128–129, p133: French+Tye
p134 (top): Nick Cavelle

First published in 2019 by Lund Humphries
Office 3, Book House
261A City Road
London EC1V 1JX
UK

www.lundhumphries.com

Brinkworth: So Good So Far
© Brinkworth and Graeme Brooker, 2019
All rights reserved

ISBN: 978-1-84822-255-7

A Cataloguing-in-Publication record for this book is available from
the British Library

Designed by FUEL

Printed in Slovenia